PC Tools Commands by Task

Task	Command or Utility
Copy disk	Copy Disk (Part 1)
Copy file	Copy File (Part 1)
Create and edit outline	Outlines (Part 2)
Create new directory	Add A Directory (Part 1)
Cut and paste data	Clipboard (Part 2)
Delete directory	Delete A Directory (Part 1)
Determine disk type and capacity	Disk Information (Part 1)
Dial telephone number	Databases (Part 2)
Edit file	Edit File (Part 1)
Edit program list	Cut, Paste, Properties (Part 1)
Fix damaged disk	DiskFix (Part 3)
Format disk	PC Format (Part 3)
Increase hard-drive access	PC-Cache, Compress (Part 3)
Locate duplicate file	File Find (Part 2)
Optimize hard disk	Compress (Part 3)
Override password	Settings (Part 1)
Print file	Print File (Part 1)

Continued on inside back cover

The Sybex Instant Reference Series

Instant References are available on these topics:

AutoCAD Release 11

dBASE

dBASE III PLUS Programming

dBASE IV Programming

dBASE IV 1.1

DESQview

DOS

DOS 5

Harvard Graphics

Harvard Graphics 3

Harvard Graphics for Windows

Lotus 1-2-3 Release 2.2

Lotus 1-2-3 Release 2.3

Lotus 1-2-3 for Windows

Macintosh Software

Microsoft Word for the Macintosh

Microsoft Word for the PC

Norton Desktop for Windows

Norton Utilities 6

PageMaker 4.0 for the Macintosh

Paradox 3.5

Windows 3.0

WordPerfect 5

WordPerfect 5.1

WordPerfect 5.1 for Windows

Computer users are not all alike. Neither are SYBEX books.

We know our customers have a variety of needs. They've told us so. And because we've listened, we've developed several distinct types of books to meet the needs of each of our customers. What are you looking for in computer help?

If you're looking for the basics, try the **ABC's** series, or for a more visual approach, select **Teach Yourself.**

Mastering and **Understanding** titles offer you a step-by-step introduction, plus an in-depth examination of intermediate-level features, to use as you progress.

Our **Up & Running** series is designed for computer-literate consumers who want a no-nonsense overview of new programs. Just 20 basic lessons, and you're on your way.

SYBEX **Encyclopedias** and **Desktop References** provide a *comprehensive reference* and explanation of all of the commands, features, and functions of the subject software.

Sometimes a subject requires a special treatment that our standard series doesn't provide. So you'll find we have titles like **Advanced Techniques, Handbooks, Tips & Tricks,** and others that are specifically tailored to satisfy a unique need.

You'll find SYBEX publishes a variety of books on every popular software package. Looking for computer help? Help Yourself to SYBEX.

For a complete catalog of our publications:

SYBEX, Inc.
2021 Challenger Drive, Alameda, CA 94501
Tel: (510) 523-8233/(800) 227-2346 Telex: 336311
Fax: (510) 523-2373

SYBEX is committed to using natural resources wisely to preserve and improve our environment. This is why we have been printing the text of books like this one on recycled paper since 1982.

This year our use of recycled paper will result in the saving of more than 15,300 trees. We will lower air pollution effluents by 54,000 pounds, save 6,300,000 gallons of water, and reduce landfill by 2,700 cubic yards.

In choosing a SYBEX book you are not only making a choice for the best in skills and information, you are also choosing to enhance the quality of life for all of us.

PC Tools™ 7.1 Instant Reference

David J. Strybel

SYBEX®

San Francisco • Paris • Düsseldorf • Soest

Acquisitions Editor: Dianne King
Series Editor: James A. Compton
Developmental Editor: Gary Masters
Editor: Richard Mills
Technical Editor: Maryann Brown
Word Processors: Ann Dunn and Susan Trybull
Series Designer: Ingrid Owen
Production Artist: Helen Bruno
Desktop Publishing Specialist: Thomas Goudie
Proofreader/Production Assistant: Janet K. Boone
Indexer: Tom McFadden
Cover Designer: Archer Design

Library of Congress Card Number: 91-67703
ISBN: 0-89588-860-2

Manufactured in the United States of America
10 9 8 7 6 5 4 3 2

To my mother and father, Josephine and Zigmunt Strybel

Acknowledgments

A team of dedicated professionals worked to develop and produce this book. At SYBEX, thanks to Gary Masters, developmental editor; Dianne King, acquisitions editor; James A. Compton, series editor; Richard Mills, editor; and Maryann Brown, technical editor. Thanks also to Debbie Hess at Central Point Software for furnishing software, and to Ken Dietz for expert technical support. A special note of thanks is extended to Gerald E. Jones for recommending me to SYBEX, as well as to Grace A. Kelley for proofreading the initial manuscript drafts.

Table of Contents

Part One

PC Shell

Part Two

Desktop Manager

Part Three

Data Recovery and System Utilities

Introduction

The idea governing this book is simple. When you come across a PC Tools 7.1 command that does not run as you intended, or if you need a quick refresher about how program menus and options work, you want a single source of information to solve your problems quickly. This book is intended to meet those needs.

This Instant Reference provides all the information you need to use PC Shell commands and Desktop Manager utilities, as well as the standalone data recovery and system utilities. The book covers menus and dialog boxes, as well as more sophisticated options. The focus of the book is PC Tools version 7.1, although some of the procedures for using commands and utilities are identical to those in earlier versions.

HOW THIS BOOK IS ORGANIZED

For ease of use, this book is divided into the following three parts:

Part One: PC Shell covers procedures for executing the commands in PC Shell, PC Tools' DOS shell.

Part Two: Desktop Manager covers procedures for running the utilities contained in the Desktop Manager, such as Notepads and Appointment Scheduler.

Part Three: Data Recovery and System Utilities covers running standalone utilities, such as DiskFix, FileFind, and Compress.

Each part consists of main entries, each of which is a command or utility. Each entry has a short overview of the command or utility, and has complete lists of steps for using it.

Many PC Tools procedures involve selections from among various options. These options are often presented under their own subheading called "Options." Occasionally, an example of actual usage of a command can be found under the subheading "Example." Miscellaneous information can be found in "Notes" sections.

You'll also find numerous tips, shortcuts, and warnings throughout the book. Helpful cross-references to related commands and utilities can be found in the "See Also" sections.

KEYBOARD AND MOUSE TECHNIQUES

This book makes no distinction between executing procedures using the keyboard or a mouse. Instead, it emphasizes the commands or items you need to select. For example, instructions such as "pull down the File menu and choose Copy" or "activate the tree list" or "in the Copy File dialog box, choose Replace All" are used.

The following table shows how to use the keyboard and mouse to carry out basic actions in PC Tools:

Procedure	Keyboard	Mouse
Activate a window or an area within a window	Press Tab repeatedly until the window is activated.	Click anywhere within the window.
Position the cursor	Activate the window, then use the arrow keys to move the cursor where you want it.	Click where you want the cursor.
Select an item	Move the cursor to the item and press Enter.	Click on the item.
Pull down a menu	Press Alt and the highlighted letter of the menu name.	Click on the menu name.

Procedure	Keyboard	Mouse
Choose a command	Move the highlight to the command and press Enter, or press the highlighted letter of the command name.	Double-click on the command name.
Scroll through the directory tree or file list	Activate the window and use Page Up or Page Down to scroll a screen at a time. Use the arrow keys to move one line or column horizontally or vertically.	Position the cursor in the window you want to scroll. Press the right mouse button and drag the mouse to the top or bottom to scroll vertically, and to the right or left to scroll horizontally.

Part One

PC Shell

PC Shell provides an interface between DOS and you, the computer user. Instead of using esoteric command entries, PC Shell allows you to manage files and programs with convenient "point-and-click" menus and dialog boxes.

This part of the book covers the major capabilities of PC Shell. It begins with a brief discussion of the various ways you can start PC Shell and run programs without exiting it. Then, the commands in PC Shell are presented, organized alphabetically, in a straightforward, step-by-step format.

OVERVIEW

PC Shell is made up of two types of commands: ones that organize files, directories, and disks and ones that organize and run programs. Depending on whether you have the file or program list activated, you will see a specific set of commands on the File menu for carrying out these tasks.

With the file list activated, you can use PC Shell to perform routine tasks, such as formatting disks, creating directories, and copying and moving files. You can also perform more advanced operations, such as editing files and recovering data.

With the program list activated, you can use PC Shell to create program items and groups. Program items describe each program and include a command line used to load it. Program groups are displayed in the program list much like directories in the file list. You can create groups to organize your programs according to function, user, or any criterion you select. For example, you might create a group called *Desktop Publishing* that includes programs like Aldus Pagemaker, Microsoft Word, Harvard Graphics, and any other programs you use for desktop publishing.

STARTING PC SHELL AS A STANDALONE APPLICATION

You can start PC Shell from the DOS prompt just as you would any DOS application. If you load it in standalone mode, PC Shell does not stay in memory when you exit. Use this option if your computer's memory is limited, or if your applications run out of memory frequently.

To Start PC Shell at the DOS Prompt

1. At the DOS prompt, type

   PCSHELL

2. Press Enter.

The screen clears. PC Shell reads the directories of the current drive. A message box tells you how many directories have been read. Then the main PC Shell screen appears.

STARTING PC SHELL AS A MEMORY-RESIDENT APPLICATION

Running PC Shell in memory-resident mode enables you to use a quick keystroke combination, or *hotkey,* to enter and quit PC Shell while running other applications. (The default is Ctrl-Esc.) In memory-resident mode, PC Shell stays in memory while other applications are run. Although switching between PC Shell and your applications is quicker, your applications may run more slowly.

The advantage of running PC Shell in memory-resident mode is that you don't have to exit your applications to perform Shell operations. For example, you can press the hotkey to leave your word processor, format a disk, copy backup files to the disk, and then return to the same place in your word processor.

You may need to experiment to determine whether running PC Shell as a memory-resident program is feasible on your machine. As a general rule, you need 470K free memory to run PC Shell in regular memory-resident mode. In tiny mode (see the /T command-line option described later), PC Shell requires only about 12K free memory, but runs considerably slower because the hard drive must be accessed frequently.

Keep in mind that if your other programs run out of memory while PC Shell is resident, you can remove it to provide more memory for those programs.

To Use PC Shell in Memory-Resident Mode

1. At the DOS prompt, type

   PCSHELL /R

2. Press Enter.
3. Press Ctrl-Esc from any application or from the DOS prompt to start PC Shell. The screen clears. PC Shell reads the directories of the current drive. A message box tells you how many directories have been read. Then the main PC Shell screen appears.
4. Press Ctrl-Esc again to exit PC Shell and return to your previous application.

• **NOTE** For systems that use extended memory (XMS) or expanded memory (EMS), you can install the SWAPSH utility to make more efficient use of available memory. With SWAPSH, the resident portion of PC Shell is loaded into upper memory, freeing up conventional memory. SWAPSH takes up about 10K of conventional memory and handles data transfers to and from PC Shell.

See Also *SWAPDT and SWAPSH* (Part 3)

STARTING PC SHELL EVERY TIME YOU BOOT YOUR COMPUTER

You can set up your system to run PC Shell every time you boot your computer. To do this, install a PC Shell command line in your AUTOEXEC.BAT file. Use the standard DOS format:

PCSHELL *options*

• **OPTIONS** Use command-line options, or *parameters*, to control the way PC Shell appears on your screen (a list appears in Table 1.1). Type them after the program name, either at the DOS prompt or in your AUTOEXEC.BAT file.

Table I.1: PC Shell Start-up Options

Option	Explanation
/25	Sets screen display to 25 lines
/28	Sets screen display to 28 lines
/43	Sets screen display to 43 lines (EGA only)
/50	Sets screen display to 50 lines (VGA only)
/A*nnn*	Allocates *nnn* K of RAM to PC Shell when run in memory-resident mode
/BF	Uses the system's BIOS to manipulate fonts
/BW	Starts PC Shell in black-and-white mode
/DQ	Disables Quick Load feature
/FF	Disables snow suppression on CGA monitors
/F*n*	Changes hotkeys to F1 through F10, where *n* is a number from 1 to 10
/IM	Disables mouse functions
/IN	Forces the color monitor selection on monochrome monitors
/LCD	Sets the monitor to LCD (usually used for laptops)
/LE	Exchanges the functions of the left and right mouse buttons
/MONO	Starts PC Shell in monochrome mode
/NF	Disables alternate fonts
/NGM	Disables graphic mouse mode (displays solid box instead of arrow)
/O*n*	Designates drive for overlay files, where *n* is the drive letter
/PS2	Resets PS/2 mouse driver
/R	Runs program in RAM-resident, or memory-resident, mode
/RL	RAM-resident large (uses about 470K of RAM)

Table I.1: PC Shell Start-up Options (continued)

Option	Explanation
/RM	RAM-resident medium (uses about 12K of RAM)
/RS	RAM-resident small (uses about 12K of RAM)
/RT	RAM-resident tiny (uses about 12K of RAM)

• EXAMPLE Suppose you want to load PC Shell on your laptop computer in memory-resident mode. Since the laptop has an LCD display, you need to set the /LCD option. Also, suppose you're left-handed, and you want to switch mouse button functions. To do all this, enter the following command line at the DOS prompt:

PCSHELL /R /LCD /LE

• NOTES Try using the /BF option if the characters on your screen look peculiar.

You can set the options described above easily by using the PC Config utility.

See Also *PC Config* (Part 3)

REMOVING PC SHELL FROM MEMORY

When PC Shell is running as a memory-resident program, you can remove it from memory at the DOS prompt or from within PC Shell.

To Unload PC Shell at the DOS Prompt

1. At the DOS prompt, type

   KILL

2. Press Enter.

To Unload PC Shell from within PC Shell

1. Pull down the **S**pecial menu.
2. Choose **R**emove PC Shell.
3. Choose **R**emove again to confirm.

RUNNING APPLICATIONS FROM PC SHELL

PC Shell gives you several options for running applications. Depending on your needs, you can run applications from any of the following:

- Program List window
- File List window
- View window
- DOS command line

You also can use the Quick Run option to speed up operations. The procedures discussed in the following section assume that you have a program list and files associated with program items. (To add groups and items to the program list, see the New command. To associate files with program items, see the Properties command.)

RUNNING PROGRAMS FROM THE PROGRAM LIST

The *program list* contains the names of all the programs you set up to run from PC Shell. When the program list is activated, the File menu contains a separate set of commands. These commands also are available from the message bar at the bottom of the screen as function-key operations.

• OPTIONS Press the corresponding function key or click the command name on the message bar to invoke these commands:

F4 (New)	Creates new menu item or group
F5 (Edit)	Edits selected program entry

F6 (Delete)	Removes selected program entry
F7 (Cut)	Moves entry to Clipboard
F8 (Copy)	Copies entry to Clipboard
F9 (Paste)	Writes Clipboard entry to new location

To Run Programs from the Program List

1. From the program list, open the program group (if any) and select the program item you want to run.
2. You can now run the program in one of four ways:
   - Press Enter.
   - Using the mouse, double-click on the program name.
   - Pull down the **F**ile menu, then choose **O**pen.
   - Pull down the **F**ile menu, then choose Laun**c**h.

• NOTE When you load a program item that has files associated with it, and one of those files is selected in the file list, PC Shell loads the file automatically with the program. Also, if the Force Launch With Selected File option is set and a file is selected, PC Shell loads the file with the program.

RUNNING PROGRAMS FROM THE FILE LIST

You can run programs from the file list in one of two ways: by selecting an executable (program) file or by selecting a data file associated with the program you want to run.

To Run an Executable File from the File List

1. Select an executable file from the file list (an executable file has the extension .BAT, .COM, or .EXE).
2. Run the program by doing either of the following:
   - Pull down the **F**ile menu and choose **O**pen.
   - Using the mouse, double-click on the file name.

3. Enter any command-line options you want to use. Choose **O**pen.

To Run a Program from an Associated File

1. From the file list, select a data file associated with a program.
2. Run the program by doing either of the following:
   - Pull down the **F**ile menu and choose **O**pen.
   - Using the mouse, double-click on the file name.
3. Enter any command-line options you want to use. Choose **O**pen.

RUNNING PROGRAMS FROM THE VIEW WINDOW

Running a program from the View window is handy if you aren't sure what file you want to use. You can use the View window to browse file contents, then run the program directly when you locate the file you need. The file must be associated with a program for this method to work.

To Run a Program from a Viewed File

1. Activate the View window.
2. Select the file you want to run. File contents are displayed in the View window.
3. Run the program by doing either of the following:
   - Press F4 or click Launch on the message bar.
   - Pull down the **F**ile menu and choose **O**pen.

RUNNING PROGRAMS FROM THE DOS COMMAND LINE

With the DOS command line turned on, you can run programs the same way you would from the DOS prompt. When you exit the program you are returned to PC Shell, unless you choose the

Wait On DOS Screen option from the Options menu. In this case, the program pauses until you hit any key.

To Run a Program from the DOS Command Line

1. Pull down the View menu.
2. Choose Custom List Configure and then DOS Command Line to turn on the DOS command line.
3. Move the cursor to the DOS command line.
4. Enter a command and its parameters.
5. Press Enter.

See Also *Custom List Configure* and *Wait On DOS Screen*

ADD A DIRECTORY

The Add A Directory command allows you to add subdirectories, or branches, to your directory tree structure.

To Create a New Directory

1. Pull down the Disk menu.
2. Choose Directory Maintenance.
3. Choose Add A Directory.
4. In the Tree List window for the current drive, select the directory to which you want to add a subdirectory. The Directory Add dialog box appears.
5. Enter the name of the new directory.
6. Choose OK to add the directory. Choose Exit to return to PC Shell.

• NOTES Directory names can be up to eight characters long and can have a three-character extension separated by a period. The name cannot contain spaces, commas, periods, or backslashes. Valid characters include the letters A through Z, the numbers 0 through 9, and the following special characters:

- Caret (^)
- Underscore (_)
- Dollar sign ($)
- Tilde (~)
- Exclamation point (!)
- Number sign (#)
- Percent sign (%)
- Ampersand (&)
- Hyphen (–)
- Braces ({ })
- Parentheses

Two subdirectories in the same directory cannot have the same name, but subdirectories in different directories can have the same name.

See Also *Directory Maintenance*

ATTRIBUTE CHANGE

The Attribute Change command allows you to change file attributes and the date and time of the last edit for selected files.

To Change File Attributes

1. From the File List window, select one or more files for which you want to change attributes.
2. Pull down the File menu.

3. Choose Change File.
4. Choose **A**ttribute Change from the Change File submenu. The files you selected are displayed in the File Attribute window.
5. Move to the file listing you want to change.
6. Choose Hidden, System, Read Only, or Archive. Use attribute keys (**H, S, R, A**) or click attribute letters to toggle file attributes off and on.
7. Move to the date and time of creation fields, and edit the entries as desired.
8. Repeat steps 5 through 7 until you have finished making changes to all files.
9. Choose **U**pdate to save your changes and return to PC Shell. Choose **C**ancel to return to PC Shell without saving your changes.

• OPTIONS The attributes you can change are the following:

Hidden: The file name is concealed and normally is not displayed in directory listings. PC Shell displays hidden files in intermediate and advanced modes.

System: The file is designated as a system file and is not affected by normal DOS operations, such as copying, deleting, moving, and so on. The file is hidden in beginner mode.

Read Only: You can only read, or view, file contents. You cannot change or edit the file.

Archive: The archive attribute indicates whether a new backup file is created at the next backup session. When the attribute is turned on, the file has been changed and is backed up at the next backup session. When turned off, a new backup file is not needed. DOS turns on the archive attribute every time a file is changed. The attribute is used by both the DOS Backup and PC Tools Backup (CP Backup) commands.

• NOTES Under normal circumstances, you should not change the system attribute of any file.

To view file attributes in the File List window, turn on the Attributes option from the File Display Options dialog box.

In Beginner User Mode, file attributes cannot be displayed.

The time and date of creation for each file is dependent on your computer's system clock. To ensure that the time and date are accurate, the system clock is either powered by battery or updated each time you boot your computer. Use the Set Date/Time command to set the system clock.

See Also *Change User Level, File Display Options,* and *Set Date/Time*

CHANGE USER LEVEL

The Change User Level command adjusts the commands displayed by PC Shell according to your skill or comfort level. The default setting is Advanced.

To Change the User Level

1. Pull down the **O**ptions menu.
2. Choose Change **U**ser Level.
3. Choose **B**eginner, **I**ntermediate, or **A**dvanced.
4. Choose **O**K.

- **OPTIONS** There are three user levels to choose from:

Beginner includes only basic DOS commands. Hidden files are not displayed.

Intermediate includes more complex functions, including deleting, editing, searching, and printing. The program list can be edited. Hidden files are displayed.

Advanced includes all DOS and PC Shell functions. Hidden files are displayed.

CLEAR FILE

The Clear File command protects the confidentiality of data by completely erasing one or more files from disk storage. (It calls the Wipe utility.)

To Clear a File

1. From the File List window, select the file or files you want to clear.
2. Pull down the **F**ile menu.
3. Choose Chan**g**e File.
4. Choose **C**lear File. The Wipe utility is loaded, and the Wiping dialog box appears.
5. Choose **S**kip, **W**ipe, or **C**ancel.
6. Repeat step 4 for all selected files. The Summary dialog box appears.
7. Choose **O**K or press Enter to exit.

Warning Once files have been cleared, they are wiped completely from storage. They cannot be recovered or read by any means. Give yourself room for error. If you want to maintain confidentiality, but not lose files, make backup copies of the files on floppy disks and store the disks securely before using Clear File to remove the files from your hard disk.

See Also *Undelete; Wipe* (Part 3)

COLLAPSE BRANCH

The Collapse Branch command hides all subdirectories, or branches, of a selected directory, or tree.

To Collapse a Branch on the Directory Tree

1. Select the directory you want to collapse.
2. Pull down the Tree menu.
3. Choose Collapse Branch.

Shortcut Directory displays can be collapsed and expanded by using the + and – keys on the numeric keypad or by clicking the directory icon to the left of the directory name.

See Also *Expand Branch*

COLORS

The Colors command allows you to change the colors displayed in different parts of the screen. (It calls the Color Options screen in PC Config.) For example, you can change the color of dialog boxes and the text displayed in them, or you can create an entirely new color scheme for PC Tools. PC Tools comes with several color schemes that you can implement easily.

To Go to the Color Options Screen

1. Pull down the Options menu.
2. Choose Colors.

To Select an Existing Color Scheme

1. From the Color Options screen, pull down the Scheme drop-down list.
2. Use the arrow keys or your mouse to move through scheme selections. Press Enter to select a color scheme. The sample screen to the right changes to show you how each scheme looks.
3. Choose OK to change your PC Tools display to the selected color scheme.

To Create a New Color Scheme

1. From the Color Options screen, pull down the File menu.
2. Choose New Scheme. The New Scheme dialog box appears.
3. Enter a name for your new color scheme in the Scheme Name text box.
4. Select a scheme to use as a template.
5. Follow the procedures described in "To Change an Existing Color Scheme."

To Change an Existing Color Scheme

1. From the Color Options screen, pull down the Scheme drop-down list.
2. Pull down the Category drop-down list, and select a category you want to change.
3. Pull down the Element drop-down list, and select an element you want to change.
4. Pull down the Color drop-down list.
5. Use the arrow keys or your mouse to select colors for Background and Foreground.
6. Repeat steps 3 and 4 for each element in the category you selected.

7. Repeat steps 2 through 4 for each category in the color scheme you selected.
8. To save the changes you have made to the color scheme, do one of the following:
   - To save the changes with the original name, pull down the **F**ile menu and choose **S**ave Scheme. Then choose **S**ave again to confirm. (You can also press F2 or click Save in the message bar at the bottom of the screen.) The new scheme is saved with the name of the existing color scheme.
   - To save the changes with a different name, pull down the **F**ile menu and choose Save Scheme **A**s. Then choose **S**ave to confirm.

See Also *PC Config* (Part 3)

COMPARE DISKS

The Compare command on the Disk menu compares a source disk to a target disk. You can do comparisons using a single drive or two drives of the same size and density. This command is useful for determining whether disk copies are identical.

To Compare Two Disks

1. Insert your source disk in the appropriate drive.
2. Pull down the **D**isk menu.
3. Choose C**o**mpare.
4. Choose the source drive (**A** or **B**).
5. Choose **O**K.
6. Choose the target drive (**A** or **B**).
7. Choose **O**K.

8. Insert the target disk in the target drive when prompted. Choose OK.
9. Follow the prompt instructions, swapping source and target disks until the comparison is completed.

Choose Cancel at any time during a comparison operation to return to PC Shell.

See Also *Compare Files*

COMPARE FILES

The Compare command on the File menu determines whether one or more pairs of files are identical. File pairs can have matching or different names, can be on the same or different disks, or can be in the same or different directories.

To Compare Files Using a Single File List Display

1. Select one or more source files for comparison.
2. Pull down the File menu.
3. Choose Compare. The File Compare dialog box appears.
4. Select the drive containing the file or files to be compared, then choose OK.
5. Choose Matching Names to compare files with the same name, or choose Different Names to compare files with different names.
6. Select the directory containing the file or files to be compared.

If you chose Matching Names, files are compared and a summary of the comparisons is displayed. Choose OK to return to PC Shell.

If you chose Different Names, follow these steps:

1. Enter the name and extension of the target file for comparison.
2. Choose OK to continue. The source and target files are displayed.
3. Choose Compare to begin the comparison. A summary of the comparison is displayed.
4. Choose OK to continue.
5. Enter the name of the next target file and compare the files. Repeat this step until all file pairs have been compared.

To Compare Files Using a Dual File List Display

1. Select one or more source files for comparison.
2. In the second file list, activate the directory that contains the target files for comparison.
3. Pull down the File menu.
4. Choose Compare. The File Compare dialog box appears.
5. Choose OK to confirm the second directory as the target path.
6. Choose Matching Names to compare files with the same name, or choose Different Names to compare files with different names.

If you chose Matching Names, the comparison begins. The comparison is summarized in the message window. Choose OK to return to PC Shell.

If you chose Different Names, follow these steps:

1. Enter the name and extension of the target file for comparison.
2. Choose OK to continue. The source and target files are displayed.
3. Choose Compare to begin the comparison. A summary of the comparison is displayed.
4. Choose OK to continue.
5. Enter the name of the next target file and compare files. Repeat this step until all file pairs have been compared.

See Also *Compare Disks*

CONFIRMATION

The Confirmation command toggles confirmation messages on and off. A confirmation message prompts you to choose Cancel to quit an operation or OK to go ahead with the operation you have chosen.

To Turn Confirmation Messages On and Off

1. Pull down the **O**ptions menu.
2. Choose **C**onfirmation.
3. Choose Confirm on **D**elete, Confirm on **R**eplace, or Confirm on **M**ouse Operations.
4. Choose **O**K.

• OPTIONS You can choose to turn confirmation messages on or off in the following circumstances:

Confirm on Delete: A confirmation message is displayed when you delete files and directories.

Confirm on Replace: A confirmation message is displayed when you replace files and directories.

Confirm on Mouse Operations: A confirmation message is displayed when you use your mouse to perform copy and move operations.

Warning Suppressing confirmation messages speeds up operations but reduces your margin for error. Turn off confirmation messages only if you are moving, copying, or deleting large numbers of files.

COPY DISK

The Copy command on the Disk menu creates a duplicate (including all files, directories, and subdirectories) of a source disk on a blank (formatted or unformatted) target disk. You can copy using a single drive or two drives of the same size and density.

To Copy a Disk

1. Pull down the **Disk** menu.
2. Choose **Copy**. The Disk Copy dialog box appears.
3. Select the source drive, which holds the disk to be copied, and choose **OK**.
4. Select the target drive, which holds the blank disk, and choose **OK**.
5. Insert the source disk as prompted, and choose **OK**.
6. Insert the target disk as prompted, and choose **OK**.

• NOTES For making copies using a single drive, you can repeat steps 5 and 6 several times.

If your target disk is unformatted, it is formatted during disk copying with the same specifications as your source disk. If your source disk contains system files, they are copied to the target disk also.

See Also *Copy File*

COPY FILE

The Copy command on the File menu copies one or more files from one drive to another, to a different directory on the same drive, or to the same directory with different names.

To Copy Files from One Location to Another

1. Select the file or files you want to copy.
2. Pull down the File menu.
3. Choose **Copy**. The File Copy dialog box appears.
4. Select the target drive.
   - If you are using the single file list display, choose the target drive (**A, B,** or **C**, for example) and choose **OK**.
   - If you are using the dual file list display, choose **OK** to confirm that that target is the drive and directory in the second file list.
5. Select the target directory, if any.

To Copy Files Using a Mouse and Dual File Lists

1. Select one or more files you want to copy.
2. In the second file list, activate the destination drive and directory.
3. Click on any selected file and drag it to the destination directory. A message box appears summarizing the copy operation.

Shortcut When the file list is activated, you can copy files quickly by pressing F5 or by clicking Copy on the message bar at the bottom of the screen.

• NOTE If you copy a file to a directory that contains a file with the identical name, the file in the destination directory will be overwritten unless you have the Confirm On Replace option turned on. When this option is turned on, you are given the following options:

Replace All: All files are copied. Files with the same names are replaced.

Replace File: One file (the file name is displayed in the dialog box) is copied. Use this option to replace files individually.

Next File: The file is not copied. The next file name is displayed.

Skip All: No files are replaced. Only files without matching names in the target directory are copied.

See Also *Confirmation*, *Copy Disk*, and *Move*

COPY (PROGRAM LIST)

You can use the Copy command with the program list activated to copy program items to the Clipboard. Items copied to the Clipboard then can be pasted in other locations on the program list.

To Copy a Program Item

1. Activate the program list.
2. Select a program group.
3. Select the program item you want to copy.
4. Pull down the **File** menu.
5. Choose **Copy**. The program item is copied to the Clipboard.

Shortcut With the program list activated, you can copy files quickly by pressing F8 or by clicking Copy on the message bar at the bottom of the screen.

• NOTES The Copy command cannot be used on program groups. To copy a program group, create a new group, then copy program items as needed to the new group.

Use the Cut command to move program items to the Clipboard (the original entries are deleted). Cut is available only when the program list is activated.

Use the Paste command to write items from the Clipboard back to the program list.

See Also *Cut* and *Paste*

CUSTOM LIST CONFIGURE

The Custom List Configure command displays a submenu of options you can use to configure your PC Shell display.

To Configure Your Display

1. Pull down the View menu.
2. Choose Custom List Configure.
3. Choose one of the options on the submenu.
4. Repeat steps 1 through 3 until PC Shell is configured the way you want it.

• **OPTIONS** The following options are available on the Custom List Configure submenu:

Tree List opens and closes the window that shows the contents of the current directory displayed as a tree structure.

File List opens and closes the window that shows the list of files contained in the current directory.

Program List opens and closes the window that shows the list of programs that can be run from PC Shell.

View Window opens and closes the window that shows the contents of a selected file.

Background Mat turns the background mat on and off.

DOS Command Line turns the DOS command line on and off.

Viewer Config toggles the orientation of the View window between horizontal and vertical.

Window Style toggles the arrangement of displayed windows between tiled and cascaded.

• **NOTE** To save your changes, click the Save Configuration check box in the Close PC Shell dialog box when you exit PC Shell, or use the Save Configuration File command on the Options menu.

See Also *Save Configuration File*

CUT (PROGRAM LIST)

Use the Cut command when you want to move program groups or items to different locations in the program list. The Cut command moves a selected group or item to the Clipboard, from which the group or item can then be pasted to another location. The Cut command is available only when the program list is activated.

To Cut a Group or an Item from the Program List

1. Activate the program list.
2. Select the program group or item you want to cut.
3. Pull down the File menu.
4. Choose Cut. Your selection is removed from the program list and written to the Clipboard.

Shortcut With the program list activated, you can cut files quickly by pressing F7 or by clicking Cut on the message bar at the bottom of the screen.

• **NOTES** Use the Copy command to copy program items to the Clipboard (original entries are not deleted).

Use the Paste command to write items from the Clipboard back to the program list.

See Also *Copy (Program List)* and *Paste*

DECRYPT FILE

The Decrypt File command decrypts, or unscrambles, one or more encrypted files, restoring them to their original, readable conditions.

To Decrypt Files

1. Select one or more encrypted files you want to decrypt.
2. Pull down the **F**ile menu.
3. Choose **S**ecure.
4. Choose **D**ecrypt File from the Secure submenu. PC Tools loads the PC Secure program.
5. Enter the password used to encrypt the file, and press Enter.
6. If the No Delete option was turned on during encryption, a dialog box appears prompting you to confirm that you want to replace the original file. Choose **O**K to replace the original, or choose **C**ancel.
7. Choose **O**K to return to PC Shell.

• **NOTE** The No Delete option is turned on by using the Settings command on the Secure submenu. If you did not delete the original file during encryption and you want to retain the original file after decryption, rename the original file before decryption.

See Also *Encrypt File* and *Settings*

DEFINE FUNCTION KEYS

The Define Function Keys command allows you to assign frequently used commands to the function keys (F1 through F10 or F12, depending on the type of keyboard you use).

To Assign Commands to Function Keys

1. Pull down the **O**ptions menu.
2. Choose Define Function **K**eys.
3. From the Current Settings list in the dialog box, select the function key you want to change.
4. From the Available Functions list, select the command you want to assign to that key.
5. Repeat steps 3 and 4 until you have reassigned all the function keys you want to reassign.
6. Choose **U**pdate to implement the changes and return to PC Shell.

• **NOTES** Your changes are not saved until you choose the Save Configuration File command, either by clicking the Save Configuration check box when exiting PC Shell or by choosing the Save Configuration File command from the Options menu. Thus, you can redefine function keys for a PC Shell session, then reset them to the default for your next session by not saving the configuration file.

The F1, F3, and F10 keys are assigned by PC Shell and cannot be redefined.

See Also *Save Configuration File*

DELETE A DIRECTORY

The Delete A Directory command on the Directory Maintenance submenu removes empty directories.

To Delete a Directory

1. Pull down the **D**isk menu.
2. Choose Directory **M**aintenance.
3. Choose **D**elete A Directory.
4. In the tree list, select the directory you want to delete.
5. Choose **OK** to confirm deletion and remove the directory, or choose Exit.

See Also *Directory Maintenance*

DELETE FILE

The Delete command on the File menu removes files from disk storage.

To Delete Files

1. Select one or more files you want to delete.
2. Pull down the **F**ile menu.
3. Choose **D**elete. The File Delete dialog box appears with the name of the first selected file.
4. Choose one of the following options:

   Delete deletes the file listed.

   Next skips the file listed and proceeds to the next selected file.

Delete All deletes all selected files without further confirmation.

The confirmation message options can be turned on and off by using the Confirmation command on the Options menu.

Warning Use caution when deleting files with .SYS, .COM, and .EXE extensions. These are system and program files; deleting them may cause your computer not to boot or your programs not to run.

See Also *Confirmation* and *Undelete*

DELETE (PROGRAM LIST)

When the program list is activated, you can use the Delete command to delete program groups or items from it.

To Delete a Program Group or Item

1. Activate the program list.
2. Select the group or item you want to remove.
3. Pull down the **File** menu.
4. Choose **Delete**.

DESKCONNECT

The DeskConnect command allows you to transfer files between two computers, such as your desktop and laptop machines. To use this command, you must connect the machines with a null modem cable (available at electronics supply stores) through your serial ports. In addition, you must install the DESKSRV and DESKCON utilities on both machines before you run DeskConnect.

To Install the DeskConnect Utilities

1. To load DESKSRV on your remote (laptop) machine, enter this command at the DOS prompt:

   DESKSRV *options*

2. To load DESKCON on your client (desktop) machine, enter this command at the DOS prompt:

   DESKCON *options*

• **OPTIONS** Enter the following command-line parameters, if needed, when loading DESKSRV and DESKCON:

/B:*nn* Sets the baud rate for transmissions. The rate can be set from 300 to 115200 baud. Standard settings are 300, 1200, 2400, 4800, 9600, and 115200 baud. Both machines must be set for the same baud rate. The default is 115200.

/C:*n* Designates the communications (serial) port you are using. You can specify COM1 through COM4. If you specify COM3 or COM4, you must set the IRQ and the address of the port with the /I and /P parameters. COM1 is the default.

/I:*n* Defines the proper hardware interrupt request (IRQ). Refer to your hardware manual for information on which IRQ your serial port uses.

/P:*nn* Defines the address of the port specified with the /C parameter.

The /U parameter unloads the utility from memory, and /? displays a help screen with all available options.

To Run DeskConnect

1. Install DESKSRV and DESKCON on your remote and local machines.
2. Load PC Shell.
3. Pull down the Special menu.

4. Choose DeskConnect.

A message box is displayed explaining that remote drives have been remapped as local drives with new designations. For example, remote drive A becomes local drive D, and remote drive C becomes local drive E. At this point, you can copy files between machines by using standard PC Shell techniques.

• NOTES DESKCON must be installed on the local machine before you load PC Shell.

Both DESKSRV and DESKCON can be installed in the AUTOEXEC.BAT files of their respective machines; however, DESKCON can be installed in one machine's AUTOEXEC.BAT file only.

Enter *KILL* at the DOS prompt to unload DESKSRV and DESKCON.

DIRECTORY MAINTENANCE

Choosing the Directory Maintenance command opens a submenu with options for navigating and performing "housekeeping" tasks on local and network drives. These tasks include creating, editing, deleting, and moving directories and subdirectories. Directory Maintenance is a standalone utility that can be called from PC Shell by choosing Full DM Program from the submenu.

See Also *Add A Directory, Delete A Directory, Modify Attributes, Prune And Graft,* and *Rename A Directory; Directory Maintenance* (Part 3)

DISK INFORMATION

The Disk Information command displays a summary of the active disk's capacity, formatting specifications, and sector allocation.

To Display Information about a Disk

1. Select the drive containing the disk for which you want information.
2. Pull down the **D**isk menu.
3. Choose Disk **I**nformation.
4. Choose **OK** to return to PC Shell.

• NOTES The Disk Information command displays the following information:

- Volume label
- Date and time of creation
- Total disk space
- Number of bytes available
- Number of bytes allocated to hidden files and the number of hidden files
- Number of bytes allocated to user files and the number of user files
- Number of bytes allocated to directories and the number of directories
- Number of bytes in bad sectors
- Number of bytes per sector
- Number of sectors per cluster
- Number of sectors per track
- Total number of clusters on the disk
- Total number of sectors on the disk

- Total number of tracks on the disk
- Number of sides on the disk
- Number of cylinders on the disk

See Also *Disk Map* and *System Info; DiskFix* (Part 3)

DISK MAP

The Disk Map command displays a map that tells you how the sectors (or clusters) on your hard disk are allocated. By looking at the map, you can determine whether your files are *fragmented* (broken up and located in random sectors on your disk). Fragmented files can cause poor system performance.

To Display a Disk Map

1. Pull down the Special menu.
2. Choose Disk Map.
3. Choose Cancel or press Escape to return to PC Shell.

• NOTES The Disk Map command uses blocks to represent disk sectors. The symbols within these blocks indicate how the sectors are allocated:

Symbol	Meaning
Shaded	Space available
. (dot)	Space allocated to user files
B	Space allocated to boot record
D	Space allocated to directory records
F	Space allocated to file allocation table (FAT)
H	Space allocated to hidden file

Symbol	Meaning
R	Space allocated to read-only file
X	Bad cluster (as marked in the FAT when the disk was formatted)

For hard disks larger than 20 or 30MB, all allocated clusters (boot record, user files, and directories) are represented by the Allocated symbol.

See Also *Disk Information* and *System Info; DiskFix* (Part 3)

DUAL FILE LISTS

The Dual File Lists command turns on and off a second set of Tree List and File List windows. Dual file lists are especially helpful when copying, moving, or comparing files located on different drives or in different directories.

To Display Dual File Lists

1. Pull down the **V**iew menu.
2. Choose **D**ual File Lists.

Shortcut To turn on dual file lists quickly, simply press Insert. To turn them off, press Delete.

See Also *Program/File Lists* and *Single File List*

EDIT FILE

The Edit File command brings up the Notepads program and is a helpful tool for creating and editing files, usually text (ASCII format) files. You can use this command to edit your CONFIG.SYS file, AUTOEXEC.BAT file, DOS batch files, or any other text file.

To Edit or Create a File

1. Select a file for editing, or go to step 2.
2. Pull down the File menu.
3. Choose Change File.
4. Choose Edit File.
5. Choose Edit to edit this file, or choose Create to a create a new file.
6. Choose Save (F2) to save your file, then choose Exit (F3) to save and exit or Exit twice to exit without changing the file.

Once you are in the file editor, enter text as you would with most word processors.

See Also *Notepads* (Part 2)

ENCRYPT FILE

The Encrypt File command protects the confidentiality of files by electronically scrambling their contents, making them unreadable until they are unscrambled, or decrypted. Encrypt produces a file with an .SEC extension.

To Encrypt Files

1. Select one or more files you want to encrypt.
2. Pull down the File menu.
3. Choose Secure.

4. Choose Encrypt File. The PC Secure utility is called up.
5. Enter a password for the selected file, and press Enter.
6. Enter the password again for verification, and press Enter. A summary of the encryption operation is displayed.
7. Choose OK to return to PC Shell.

• NOTES The first time you use PC Secure, you are prompted to create a *master key*. The master key is used to override passwords for encrypted files (in advanced mode). Do not lose or forget your passwords or your master key.

Use the Decrypt File command to unscramble encrypted files. Use the Settings command to set options for encryption.

See Also *Decrypt File* and *Settings; PC Secure* (Part 3)

EXPAND ALL

The Expand All command shows all the directories that are on a selected drive.

To Expand All Directories on a Drive

1. Pull down the Tree Menu.
2. Choose Expand All.

Shortcut To expand all directories quickly, position the highlight at the root directory and press the asterisk (*) key.

EXPAND BRANCH

The Expand Branch command uncovers all hidden subdirectories, or branches, of a selected directory, or tree.

To Expand a Branch

1. Select the directory you want to expand.
2. Pull down the **T**ree menu.
3. Choose Expand **B**ranch.

Shortcut Current directories and subdirectories can be quickly collapsed and expanded by pressing the + and – keys on the numeric keypad or by clicking the directory icon to the left of the directory name.

See Also *Collapse Branch*

EXPAND ONE LEVEL

The Expand One Level command shows the next level, or branch, in a directory tree.

To Expand a Directory One Level

1. Move the highlight to the directory you want to expand.
2. Pull down the **T**ree menu.
3. Choose E**x**pand One Level.

Shortcut To expand a directory quickly, click the + symbol next to the directory name or press the + key on the numeric keypad. (The + symbol indicates hidden branches for a directory; the – symbol indicates that all branches are displayed.)

FILE DISPLAY OPTIONS

The File Display Options command allows you to specify display elements and sort sequences for the file list. You can display any combination of file names, sizes, attributes, and time/date of creation. You can also sort files according to name, extension, size, and date/time.

To Change File Display Options

1. Pull down the **O**ptions menu.
2. Choose **F**ile Display Options. The Display Options dialog box appears.
3. Choose options.
4. Choose **OK** to return to PC Shell.

• OPTIONS File Display Options allows you to select from three sets of options. You can select one Sort By option, one Sort Direction option, and one or more What To Display options.

These are the Sort By options:

Name: Files are sorted alphabetically by file name.

Extension: Files are sorted alphabetically by file extension.

Size: Files are sorted according to size.

Date/Time: Files are sorted according to date and time of creation.

None: Files are not sorted.

These are the What To Display options:

Size: Sizes of files are displayed, in bytes.

Date: Dates of creation are displayed.

Time: Times of creation are displayed.

Attribute: File attributes (hidden, system, read-only, and archive) are displayed.

Number of Clusters: Number of clusters occupied by files is displayed.

These are the Sort Direction options:

Ascending: Files are sorted alphabetically from A to Z, by date from oldest to newest, or by size from smallest to largest.

Descending: Files are sorted in reverse alphabetical order from Z to A, by date from newest to oldest, or by size from largest to smallest.

See Also *File List Filter* and *File Select Filter*

FILE LIST FILTER

The File List Filter command displays files selectively, according to common file names, extensions, or characters.

To Display File Groups with the File List Filter

1. Activate the directory from which you want to display a filtered group of files.
2. Pull down the View menu.
3. Choose Filters.
4. Choose File List.
5. Enter the file name (or partial name) and extension you want to use as a filter. Use the * wildcard to specify an entire name or a group of characters. Use the ? wildcard to specify individual characters. For example, to list all files with .DOC extensions, enter * in the Name box and *DOC* in the Extension box.

• OPTIONS The following options are available in the File List Filter dialog box:

Display returns you to the PC Shell directory window. Files are displayed according to parameters specified in step 5 above.

Reset changes the Name and Extension settings back to the default (*.*).

Cancel quits the Filter operation and returns you to PC Shell.

See Also *File Display Options* and *File Select Filter*

FILE MAP

The File Map command displays a map that shows you how individual files are allocated to sectors (or clusters) on your hard disk. In this way, you can determine whether your files are *fragmented* (broken up and located in random sectors on your disk). Fragmented files can cause poor system performance.

To Display a File Map

1. Select the files that you want to map.
2. Pull down the **S**pecial menu.
3. Choose **F**ile Map.

• NOTES The File Map command uses blocks to represent disk clusters. The symbols within these blocks indicate how clusters are allocated.

Symbol	Meaning
Shaded	Space available
. (dot)	Space allocated to user files
B	Space allocated to boot record

Symbol	Meaning
D	Space allocated to directory records
F	Space allocated to file allocation table (FAT)
H	Space allocated to hidden file
R	Space allocated to read-only file
X	Bad cluster (as marked in the FAT when the disk was formatted)

For disks larger than 20 or 30MB, all allocated clusters (boot record, user files, and directories) are represented by the Allocated symbol.

See Also *Disk Information*, *Show Information*, and *System Info*

FILE SELECT FILTER

The File Select Filter command selects groups of files from the active directory that have common file names, extensions, or characters.

To Select a Group of Files with the File Select Filter

1. Activate the directory from which you want to select a filtered group of files.
2. Pull down the View menu.
3. Choose Filters.
4. Choose File Select.
5. Enter filter parameters, using the file name (or partial name) and extension you want to use to group files. Use the * wildcard to represent an entire name or group of characters. Use the ? wildcard to represent individual characters. For example, to select files named PART1, PART2, PART2A, PART2B, PART3, and so on, enter *PART** in the Name box and * in the Extension box.

• OPTIONS The following options are available in the File Select Filter dialog box:

> **Display** returns you to PC Shell. Files are automatically selected according to parameters specified in step 5 above.
>
> **Reset** sets the default Name and Extension settings (*.*) in the dialog box.
>
> **Cancel** closes the dialog box and returns you to PC Shell.

Shortcut To access the File Select Filter dialog box quickly, press F9 or click Select in the message bar at the bottom of the PC Shell screen.

See Also *File Display Options* and *File List Filter*

FORMAT DATA DISK

The Format Data Disk command is used to format a nonsystem disk. It calls the PC Format utility.

All new disks must be formatted before they can be used to store data. Formatting a disk initializes its tracks and sectors so that they can be read from and written to by DOS. In addition, you can format a disk if you want to erase everything on it.

Using the Format Data Disk command in PC Shell allows you to set options that increase your chances of recovering data from the disk if you accidentally format it.

To Format a Data (Nonsystem) Disk

1. Pull down the **D**isk menu.
2. Choose **F**ormat Data Disk.
3. Choose the drive holding the disk you want to format (usually A or B), then choose **OK**.

4. Choose formatting options (discussed in "Options").
5. Select the desired density for the formatted disk (floppy disks only).
6. Choose **OK**. If there are files on the disk, they are listed in a window.
7. Choose **OK** to continue (formatting begins) or choose Cancel. After formatting is complete, choose **OK**.
8. Repeat steps 4 through 7 to format another disk.
9. To exit PC Format, choose **Cancel**, then **Exit**, then **OK**.

• OPTIONS

The formatting options are the following:

Safe Format formats the disk so that its files can be recovered with Unformat if necessary.

Quick Format can be used on Bernoulli boxes and RAM disks. This selection erases the root directory and file allocation table (FAT) but does not erase data or check media sectors.

Full Format formats each disk sector. The root directory and FAT are cleared.

Destructive Format formats a disk so that files cannot be recovered. All tracks and directories and the FAT are erased.

Install System Files copies system files onto the formatted disk. The resulting disk is bootable.

Save Mirror Info improves the chances for recovery if the Mirror utility has been run on disk.

Label creates a volume label (11 characters is the maximum) for your disk.

Warning Once you save files on a disk, you lose data in the sectors in which those files are written. These sectors cannot be recovered.

The Unformat program is designed to recover files from disks that have been formatted. However, it is not foolproof. When formatting disks, use extreme caution not to format disks containing important files. Make backups of disks and files you may need later.

See Also *Make Disk Bootable; Mirror* and *PC Format* (Part 3)

HEX EDIT FILE

The Hex Edit File command calls up the hex editor, which you can use to edit binary files. Binary files are distinguishable by .OBJ, .EXE, .COM, and .BIN extensions.

To Display the Hex Editor

1. Select the file or files you want to edit.
2. Pull down the File menu.
3. Choose Change File.
4. Choose Hex Edit File.

To Edit a File with the Hex Editor

1. On the File Edit screen, choose Edit from the message bar or press F7.
2. Move the cursor to the area you want to change.
3. Enter new hexadecimal values.
4. To save your changes, choose Save from the message bar or press F5.
5. To exit, choose Exit from the message bar or press F3.

• OPTIONS The following commands are available from the File Edit screen. To invoke one of them, press the corresponding function key or click on the command in the message bar at the bottom of the screen.

F1 (Help)	Displays context-sensitive help screens with information about the command or feature you're using
F2 (Index)	Displays an index of available help topics
F3 (Exit)	Quits File Edit and returns you to PC Shell

F5 (ASCII/Hex)	Toggles between hex and ASCII screen display
F6 (Sector)	Allows you to choose a different relative sector in the file
F7 (Edit)	Changes to Sector Edit screen and allows you to enter changes
F9 (NextF)	Displays the next selected file

The following commands are available from the Sector Edit screen (used to repair bad sectors). To invoke one of them, press the corresponding function key or click on the command in the message bar at the bottom of the screen.

F1 (Help)	Displays context-sensitive help screens with information about the command or feature you're using
F2 (Index)	Displays an index of available help topics
F3 (Exit)	Quits Sector Edit and returns you to PC Shell
F5 (Save)	Saves changes and rewrites the sector to reflect your edit
F8 (Asc/hx)	Toggles between ASCII and hex screen display

HIDE ALL LISTS

The Hide All Lists command turns off all windows and menus and activates the DOS command line. This command allows you to view underlying programs (provided the background mat has been turned off) and to clear the screen before you perform DOS operations.

To Turn Off All PC Shell Windows and Pull-Down Menus

1. Pull down the View menu.

2. Choose Hide All Lists.

Press F10 or click on Menu in the message bar to redisplay the menus and windows.

• NOTES All PC Shell commands are still available when windows and pull-down menus are hidden. Use the Alt key to pull down hidden menus. The message bar remains visible at the bottom of the screen. Press function keys or click on command names to invoke these commands.

Use the Custom List Configure command to turn off the background mat.

See Also *Custom List Configure*

LAUNCH (PROGRAM LIST)

The Launch command allows you to load programs and associated files automatically. This command is available only when the program list is activated.

To Load a Program and File

1. From the file list, select the file you want to load.
2. Activate the program list, and select the program you want to load.
3. Pull down the File menu.
4. Choose Launch, or press Ctrl-Enter.

Shortcut You can launch a program with an associated file quickly by using one of these two methods:

- Select the file and press Ctrl-Enter.
- Using the mouse, double-click on the file.

• **NOTE** The Launch command can be used only with files associated with programs. Use the Properties command to make associations between files and programs.

See Also *Properties*

LOCATE

The Locate command on the File menu locates one or more files according to parameters you specify. (It calls the FileFind utility.) You can locate files by name, text strings within files, date, size, attributes, directories, and user-defined groups. You also can find duplicate files, and compare and view located files.

To Locate a File or Group of Files

1. Activate the drive on which you want to search for files.
2. Pull down the **F**ile menu.
3. Choose **L**ocate.
4. To search according to file name and extension, move to the File **S**pecification box, and enter the desired name and extension.
5. To search according to text strings within files, move to the **C**ontaining box, and enter the desired text string. Choose **I**gnore Case to search for a text string regardless of whether it is in upper- or lowercase letters. Choose **W**hole Word to search for the text string only when it appears as a whole word.
6. To find duplicate files, pull down the **S**earch menu, and choose Find **D**uplicates. The Duplicate Search Status window appears.
7. To begin the search, choose the Start button (press Alt-T), or pull down the **S**earch menu and choose Star**t**.

To Specify a Directory for the Search

1. Choose the Drives button (press Alt-R), or pull down the Search menu and choose Selected Drives.
2. Choose a directory option:

   Entire Drive searches all directories of the current drive.

   Current Directory and Below searches the current directory and subdirectories below it.

   Current Directory Only searches only the current directory.

To Specify a Group of Files for the Search

1. Choose the Group button (press Alt-G), or pull down the Search menu and choose Groups.
2. Choose Search Group options:
   - To select a search group, move the highlight to the group you want to select. Choose OK to return to the Search Drives window. The File Specification box displays characteristics (name and extension parameters) for the search group.
   - To edit the characteristics of a group, choose Edit. Enter new file specifications, then choose Save to save your changes.
   - To create a new search group, choose Edit. Enter a new name and file specifications, then choose Save to save your new group.

To Search according to File Attributes, Date/Time of Creation, or Size

1. Choose the Filters button (press Alt-L), or pull down the Search menu and choose Filters. The Search Filters dialog box appears.
2. To specify file attributes as search parameters:
   - Move to the attribute box: Read-Only, System, Hidden, or Archive. Press Enter, or simply click on the

selection boxes of attributes you want to use as search parameters.

- Select options: Only These Attributes or Including These Attributes.

3. To specify date/time of last modification as the search parameters:
   - Choose **M**odified After. Enter the date and time.
   - Move to the Before boxes, and enter the date and time.
4. To specify size as a search parameter, choose Si**z**e. Define Greater Or Less Than parameters by entering desired sizes in the appropriate boxes.
5. Once you have selected parameters, choose **OK** to proceed. Or choose **R**eset to clear your selections from the File Specifications box. Choose Cancel to return to the FileFind screen.

See Also *FileFind* (Part 3)

MAKE DISK BOOTABLE

The Make Disk Bootable command formats a disk and installs the operating system files needed to start your computer.

To Format a Bootable (System) Disk

1. Pull down the **D**isk menu.
2. Choose Make Disk **B**ootable.
3. Select the drive to format, then choose **OK**.
4. Select a format density for the selected drive, then choose **OK**.

• NOTES When you install PC Tools, you are asked whether you want to create a *recovery disk*. A recovery disk is a bootable disk that contains your CONFIG.SYS and AUTOEXEC.BAT files, as well as the MIRROR file that can be used to recover files from your hard disk in the event of failure. Always make and keep a recovery disk for emergencies.

The Unformat command can recover disks that have been formatted. However, it is not foolproof. When formatting disks, use extreme caution not to erase important files and data.

See Also *Format Data Disk; PC Format* (Part 3)

MEMORY MAP

The Memory Map command displays information about how your system uses its conventional and upper memory areas. This command allows you to learn the type, location, and size of DOS memory blocks and the names of the applications occupying them.

To Display the Conventional Memory Map

1. Pull down the Special menu.
2. Choose Memory Map.
3. Use the command buttons to display additional information.
4. Choose **OK** to return to PC Shell.

• **OPTIONS** The Conventional Memory Information message window gives you the following options for displaying additional memory information:

List toggles with Graph and displays memory allocation as a list of file names and sizes.

Graph toggles with List and displays memory allocation as a graph of stacked bars.

Details toggles with Summary and provides information about the component parts of your files. For example, a system file might be broken down to show how much space is allocated to HIMEM.SYS, the mouse driver, files, buffers, and so on.

Summary toggles with Details and provides summary information about file allocation.

Statistics provides information about conventional memory, including total conventional memory, free conventional memory, largest free block, and memory allocation strategy.

Extended provides extended memory information, including driver version, bytes available, HMA (High Memory Area) status, and BIOS data.

Expanded displays the expanded memory information.

See Also *Disk Information* and *System Info; System Information* (Part 3)

MODIFY ATTRIBUTES

The Modify Attributes command on the Directory Maintenance submenu changes directory attributes: hidden, system, read-only, and archive. (It calls the Directory Maintenance utility.) Changing a directory's attributes affects the way it is displayed and may prevent you from writing to that directory.

To Change the Attributes of a Directory

1. Pull down the **D**isk menu.
2. Choose Directory **M**aintenance.
3. Choose **M**odify Attributes.
4. In the tree list for the current drive, select the directory you want to modify. The Modify Directory Attributes dialog box appears.
5. Choose **H**idden, **S**ystem, **R**ead Only, or **A**rchive.

6. Choose **Update** to save your changes, or choose **Cancel** to return to PC Shell.

• OPTIONS In the Modify Directory Attributes dialog box, you can choose from the following attributes:

Hidden: The directory is concealed from the DIR command in DOS and from PC Shell in beginner mode. The directory is visible in Directory Maintenance.

System: The directory is concealed from the DIR command in DOS and from PC Shell in beginner mode. The directory is visible in Directory Maintenance. Under normal circumstances, this attribute is not used.

Read Only: Files in this directory are protected. They cannot be modified, erased, or renamed; they can only be viewed.

Archive: Under normal circumstances, this option is not used. It may be used for some copy protection schemes.

• NOTES The root directory has no attributes.

Network directory attributes cannot be changed.

Changing the attributes of system directories can prevent your hard drive from booting. In addition, many programs create temporary files or write to data files as they are run. Changing attributes of program directories may affect their ability to run properly.

See Also *Directory Maintenance* (Part 3)

MOVE

The Move command on the File menu moves one or more files from one disk to another or to a different directory on the same disk. Use the single file list display to move files from one directory to another on the same disk. Use the dual file list display to move files to a different disk.

To Move Files Using a Single List Display

1. Select one or more files you want to move.
2. Pull down the **File** menu.
3. Choose **Move**.
4. Choose **OK** to confirm the move operation.
5. Select the destination drive (use the arrow keys or mouse), then choose **OK**.
6. If the destination drive contains subdirectories, the tree list is displayed. Select the destination directory.

To Move Files Using a Dual List Display

1. From the first file list, select one or more files you want to move.
2. Press Insert to activate the second file list, and select the drive and directory to which you want to move files.
3. Pull down the **File** menu.
4. Choose **Move**.
5. Choose **OK** to confirm the move operation.
6. Choose **OK** to confirm the second file list directory as the destination for the move.

To Move Files Using the Mouse and a Dual File List Display

1. From the first file list, select one or more files that you want to move.
2. In the second file list, activate the directory to which you want to move the files.

3. While holding down the Ctrl key, click and drag selected files from the first file list to the destination directory in the second file list. A message window shows you how many files are being moved.

• OPTIONS If files with the same name are in the destination drive or directory, you are given the following options in the File Move dialog box:

Replace All replaces all files with the same names.

Replace File replaces one file at a time (the file name is displayed in the dialog box).

Next File skips the file and moves to the next file.

Skip All moves only files with names that do not exist already on the destination drive or directory.

These options are available only when Confirm On Replace and Confirm On Mouse Operations (when you are using a mouse) are turned on. Turn on confirmation messages by using the Confirmation command on the Options menu.

See Also *Copy File*

NEW (PROGRAM LIST)

The New command allows you to add program groups and items to your program list. This command is available only when the program list is activated.

To Add a Program Group or Item to the Program List

1. Activate the program list.
2. Pull down the File menu.
3. Choose New. The New Menu Item box appears.

4. Choose **Group** if you want to add a program group, or choose **Item** if you want to add a program item.
5. Choose **OK**. The Program Group Information or Program Item Information dialog box appears.
6. Enter Title, Password (if desired), and Description for the group or item. Descriptions are displayed for selected entries in Program List Only mode.
7. Choose **OK** to save your changes and return to the program list. The new group or item appears in the list.

Tip You can add existing program items to a new group by using the Cut and Paste commands on the File menu.

See Also *Cut, Paste, Program List Only,* and *Properties*

OPEN

The Open command on the File menu allows you to run programs from the file list or program list. You can use this command in several ways:

- With the file list activated, you can run programs by selecting program files (which have .COM, .EXE, and .BAT extensions).
- With the file list activated, you can run files associated with programs. Programs and files are both loaded automatically.
- With the program list activated, you can open program groups and run program items.
- With the program list activated and an associated file selected in the file list, you can open a program and a file automatically.

When you exit programs run using this command, you are returned to PC Shell, provided PC Shell is running as a memory-resident program.

To Run a Program Using the Open Command

1. In the file list, select the program you want to run (usually designated by an .EXE, a .COM, or a .BAT extension).
2. Pull down the **File** menu.
3. Choose **Open**.
4. Enter command-line options for the program, if any.
5. Choose **Open**.

Shortcut There are two easier ways you can run programs from the file list or program list:

- Move the highlight to the program file and press Enter.
- Using the mouse, double-click on the program file.

• NOTE You can make file/program associations through the Program Item Information dialog box, which you can get to by choosing the New or Properties command.

See Also *New* and *Properties*

PARK DISK HEADS

The Park Disk Heads command moves the read/write head of your hard drive to an unused portion of the disk and prevents data loss caused by the head touching the disk surface. Use this command before shutting off or moving your computer.

To Park a Disk

1. Pull down the Disk menu.

2. Choose Park Disk Heads.
3. Your disk heads are parked. Turn off your computer without exiting PC Shell.

To Park Multiple Disks

1. Select the drive for the disk you want to park first.
2. Pull down the Disk menu.
3. Choose Park Disk Heads.
4. Repeat steps 1–3 for the next drive you want to park. (Make sure that you park the disk containing PC Tools last.)
5. Your disk heads are parked. Turn off your computer without exiting PC Shell.

Warning Make sure to exit any underlying applications before you park the heads and turn off your computer.

PASTE (PROGRAM LIST)

The Paste command writes the contents of the Clipboard to the program list. You should first use the Cut or Copy command to write program groups or items to the Clipboard. The Paste command is available from the File menu only when the program list is activated.

To Paste the Contents of the Clipboard to the Program List

1. Position the highlight bar in the location where you want to place the program entry.
2. Pull down the File menu.
3. Choose Paste.

See Also *Cut* and *Copy (Program List)*

PRINT FILE

The Print File command prints the contents of one or more files. Files are sent to the LPT1 port for printing and are printed unformatted as standard ASCII characters unless specified otherwise.

To Print Files

1. Select one or more files you want to print.
2. Pull down the **F**ile menu.
3. Choose **P**rint.
4. Choose Print **F**ile. The File Print dialog box appears.
5. Specify print options:

   Print as a Standard Text File prints standard ASCII characters, unformatted.

   Print File Using PC Shell Print Options prints standard ASCII characters and lets you define the page layout (see "Options").

   Dump Each Sector in ASCII and Hex prints both ASCII characters and the hexadecimal values of all characters in the file.

6. Choose **N**ext from the File Print dialog box to skip the current file and to go to the next selected file.
7. Choose **P**rint to print the file.

• **OPTIONS** If you choose Print File Using PC Shell Print Options, a second File Print dialog box appears. Enter values in the appropriate space for each option, or click on the ↑ and ↓ symbols to increase or decrease the displayed values.

Lines per Page sets the number of lines on each page.

Extra Spaces Between Lines sets the number of blank lines between lines of text. A value of 1 prints double-spaced text.

Margin Lines Top and Bottom sets the number of lines for top and bottom margins.

Left Margin sets the number of spaces for the left margin.

Right Margin sets the number of spaces for the right margin, starting from the left (if the entire page is 85 spaces, a value of 80 produces a margin five spaces from the right).

Page Header prints header text on each page (32 characters maximum).

Page Footer prints footer text on each page (32 characters maximum).

Page Settings sets a series of options: Page Headers, Page Footers, Page Numbers (prints at bottom of page), Stop Between Pages, and Eject Last Page.

PRINT FILE LIST

The Print File List command prints a summary of the files listed in the current directory. The printed list includes the name, size, number of disk clusters, date, time, and attributes for each file in the selected directory, and the total number of files and bytes in the directory.

To Print a File List

1. Pull down the File menu.
2. Choose Print.
3. Choose Print File List.

• **NOTE** The Print File List command prints the entire contents of the selected directory, even if you have used File Display Options or File List Filter to alter the display.

PROGRAM/FILE LISTS

The Program/File Lists command displays both the file and program lists. The program list is activated automatically.

To Turn Program/File Lists On and Off

1. Pull down the **V**iew menu.
2. Choose Program/**F**ile Lists.

See Also *Dual File Lists* and *Single File List*

PROGRAM LIST ONLY

The Program List Only command sets a PC Shell mode that activates the Program List window, closes all File List windows, and turns off the pull-down menus. In this mode, you can open program groups, run program items, edit program item information, and display program descriptions.

To Set PC Shell to Program List Only

1. Pull down the **V**iew menu.
2. Choose **P**rogram List Only.
3. When the program list is active, press F10 or click Shell on the message bar to return to PC Shell.

See Also *Overview: Running Applications from PC Shell*

PROPERTIES (PROGRAM LIST)

The Properties command allows you to edit stored information about the groups and items in your program list. This information is saved when you create or install program groups or items. Program group information consists of a name, a password (if any), and a short text description of the group. You can manipulate program item information to do the following:

- Enter program commands and options
- Identify program directories
- Associate files with programs
- Enter keystrokes for the command line
- Control the way your programs are loaded from PC Shell

To Edit Program Group Information

1. Activate the program list.
2. Select the program group you want to edit.
3. Pull down the **F**ile menu.
4. Choose **P**roperties. The Program Group Information dialog box appears.
5. Enter the name of the group in the Title field.
6. Enter a password, if desired, in the Password field.
7. To create a description entry for the group, choose **D**escription. A Notepads File Editor window appears. Enter a description. Press F2 or click on Save in the message bar to save your changes to the description and close the window.
8. Choose **OK** to save your changes and return to PC Shell, or choose Cancel to return to PC Shell without saving your changes.

To Edit Program Item Information

1. Activate the program list.
2. Select the program item you want to edit.
3. Pull down the **File** menu.
4. Choose **Properties**. The Program Item Information dialog box appears.
5. Enter the name of the item in the Program Title field.
6. In the Commands field, enter the command line you want to use to execute the program. Include the full path name (unless the path is specified in your AUTOEXEC.BAT file) and any slash commands or options you want to include. (See the "Options" section for more information on this field.)
7. In the Startup Directory field, enter the drive and directory containing the program files for the program. (See the "Options" section for more information on this field.)
8. Enter a password, if desired, in the Password field.
9. To create a description entry for the group, choose **Description**. A Notepads File Editor window appears. Enter the description. Press F2 or click on Save in the message bar to save your changes to the description and close the window. Program descriptions are displayed only when PC Shell is in Program List Only mode.
10. Choose **Advanced** to configure the following:

    User Prompt creates a text string that is displayed before the program starts. For example, you might enter a reminder to insert a disk you need to run the program. When your prompt is displayed, PC Shell pauses until you press any key.

    File Associations sets specifications for the files you want to associate with the program. Use the ? wildcard to represent individual characters and the * wildcard to represent groups of characters. For example, enter **.DOC* to associate all files with .DOC extensions to Microsoft Word.

You must associate files to be able to load them automatically when running programs from PC Shell.

Keystrokes records a sequence of keystrokes used to start the program. For example, when loading WordPerfect 5.1 you might enter <F5> at the end of your command line to execute the List Files command when the program is loaded.

Quick Run turns on Quick Run mode for individual programs.

Exit to DOS after Application sets PC Shell to go to DOS when you exit the program instead of returning to PC Shell.

Force Launch with Selected File enables you to start the program and automatically load the first highlighted file in the file list, even if the file is not associated with the program.

Don't Clear Screen before Launch tells PC Shell not to clear the screen before starting the program.

This is a PC Tools Application designates the program as part of the PC Tools group.

11. Choose **OK** to save your changes and exit the Advanced Program Item Information dialog box.

12. Choose **OK** again to save your changes and exit the Program Item Information dialog box.

• OPTIONS With the Program Item Information dialog box open, you can use the F7 and F8 function keys to facilitate making entries in the Commands, Startup Directory, User Prompt, and Keystrokes fields (the last two are available in the Advanced dialog box).

The F7 (Litkey) key tells PC Shell to interpret keystrokes literally. For example, if you press F7 and Escape, <esc> appears in the field you have selected. Pressing F7 first tells PC Shell to interpret this as the Escape key rather than <, e, s, c, >. Use this method when entering Ctrl, Shift, Esc, Alt, and function keys (F1 through F12).

The F8 (Keyword) key displays a list of frequently used keywords that can be inserted in these fields. To do this, select the keywords you want to insert, then choose Insert. The selections you make specify entries for the selected field. For example, suppose you associate all files with .DOC extensions with the WordPerfect program item in your program list. In the Commands field, you insert the <Path> keyword after your command line. Then, by selecting any file with a .DOC extension and running WordPerfect from PC Shell, the selected file is loaded automatically. Notice that the full path and file name are added to the DOS command line when the program is run.

Tip When entering title names for program groups or items, you can specify a command letter by inserting the caret symbol (^) before the letter you want to use. This letter appears in boldface in the program list, and the program group or item can be opened simply by pressing that letter. For example, enter *Word^Perfect* in the Program Title field for your WordPerfect entry. With the program list activated, pressing P loads the WordPerfect program.

See Also *New*

PRUNE AND GRAFT

The Prune And Graft command on the Directory Maintenance submenu allows you to move a directory branch, with all its subdirectories and files, to another location in the directory tree.

To Move a Directory, Subdirectories, and Files

1. Pull down the **D**isk menu.
2. Choose Directory **M**aintenance.
3. Choose **P**rune And Graft.

4. In the tree list for the current drive, select the directory you want to move, or prune.
5. In the Directory Prune And Graft dialog box, confirm the selected directory by choosing **OK**. Choose Exit to return to PC Shell.
6. Select the branch to which you want to attach, or graft, the directory.
7. To confirm the grafting operation, choose **OK**. Choose Exit to return to PC Shell.

See Also *Directory Maintenance* (Part 3)

QUICK RUN

The Quick Run command allows you to turn the Quick Run option on and off. When Quick Run is on, PC Shell does not free up memory before running programs. Programs start faster because no memory swapping takes place. Turn off the Quick Run option if your programs run out of memory or run exceptionally slow.

To Turn Quick Run On or Off

1. Pull down the **O**ptions menu.
2. Choose **Q**uick Run.

• **NOTE** The Quick Run option is available only when PC Shell is running in memory-resident mode.

See Also *Overview: Running Applications from PC Shell*

REFRESH

The Refresh command rereads the directory tree of the current drive. When PC Shell reads a directory tree, it saves a copy of the tree and reads the copy instead of the tree. This speeds operations, but the saved information is displayed even if you switch floppies or change the sort order of directories. Using the Refresh command keeps the file list current.

To Reread the Directory Tree

1. Pull down the **V**iew menu.
2. Choose **R**efresh.

See Also *Sort Files In Directory*

RENAME A DIRECTORY

The Rename A Directory command changes the name of an existing directory.

To Change the Name of a Directory

1. Pull down the **D**isk menu.
2. Choose Directory **M**aintenance.
3. Choose **R**ename A Directory. The Directory Rename dialog box appears.
4. Select the directory you want to rename.
5. Enter the new name and extension for the selected directory.

6. Choose **OK** to rename the directory, or choose Exit to return to PC Shell.

See Also *Directory Maintenance* (Part 3)

RENAME FILE

The Rename command on the File menu changes the name of one or more files.

To Rename Files

1. Select one or more files you want to rename.
2. Pull down the **F**ile menu.
3. Choose Re**n**ame. If you selected one file, go to step 5.
4. The Global File Rename dialog box appears. Choose an option:

   Global renames all files with the same name or extension (not both).

   Single renames files individually.
5. The File Rename dialog box appears. Enter the new name and extension for each file. Choose **N**ext File to skip the current file and to go to the next one.
6. Choose **R**ename.

RENAME VOLUME

The Rename Volume command changes the volume name assigned to a disk.

To Rename a Volume

1. Select the drive you want to rename.
2. Pull down the **D**isk menu.
3. Choose **R**ename Volume. The Disk Rename dialog box appears.
4. Enter the new volume label (up to 11 characters).
5. Choose **R**ename.

RUN

The Run command displays a dialog box you can use to enter and run DOS commands without leaving PC Shell. This command is available only when the file list is activated. If you use this command to run a program, you are returned to PC Shell when you exit.

To Run a DOS Command from PC Shell

1. Pull down the **F**ile menu.
2. Choose **R**un. The Run DOS Command dialog box appears.
3. Enter a DOS command just as you would at the DOS prompt.
4. Choose **OK** to run the command.
5. Press any key or click once to return to PC Shell.

• **NOTE** Using the Open and Launch commands, you can run programs and automatically load associated files.

See Also *Open* and *Launch*

SAVE CONFIGURATION FILE

The Save Configuration File command saves all PC Shell configuration settings, such as screen colors, program lists, viewed windows, and the current drive. When you save the configuration file, all settings are current the next time you load the program, even when your computer has been turned off. These settings are saved in a file named PCSHELL.CFG, which usually can be found in the \PCTOOLS or \PCTOOLS\DATA directory.

To Save Your Configuration Settings

1. Pull down the **O**ptions menu.
2. Choose S**a**ve Configuration File.

• NOTES When you exit PC Shell by choosing Exit from the File menu, you are given the option to save configuration settings before the program is closed.

Use the Custom List Configure and Define Function Keys commands to change PC Shell's configuration settings.

The PC Config utility contains all the PC Shell configuration options.

See Also *Custom List Configure* and *Define Function Keys; PC Config* (Part 3)

SEARCH DISK

The Search command on the Disk menu searches a disk (including deleted files) for a string of up to 32 characters, in either ASCII or hexadecimal format. Once the string is located, you can view it or edit it with the hex editor.

To Search a Disk for a Character String

1. Pull down the **Disk** menu.
2. Choose **Search**. The Disk Search dialog box appears.
3. Enter a character string (ASCII) for your search. To search for hexadecimal strings, choose **Hex** and enter the hexadecimal values. For example, enter *50 43* to search for the string *PC*.
4. Choose **OK** to begin the search, or choose **Cancel** to return to PC Shell.
5. When an occurrence of the string is found, choose one of these options:

   OK resumes the search.

   Name displays the names of files containing the search string.

   Edit displays the hex editor; the cursor will be positioned at the first byte matching the string.

   Cancel ends the search and returns you to PC Shell.

Tip By searching for hexadecimal strings, you can locate control characters and graphics characters.

See Also *Search Files*

SEARCH FILES

The Search command on the File menu searches files for character strings up to 32 characters long, in either ASCII or hexadecimal format. You can search all files in the active window, selected files in the window, or unselected files. You are also given the option of editing located files with the hex editor.

To Search Files

1. Activate the file list from which you want to search files.
2. If you want to search only selected files, select one or more files you want to search.
3. Pull down the **File** menu.
4. Choose Search. The Text Search dialog box appears.
5. Enter the search string. Choose **Hex** to enter the string in hexadecimal format.
6. Choose one of the Search options:

   All Files searches all files in the current window.

   Selected Files searches only selected files.

   Unselected Files searches only unselected files.
7. Choose one of the If Found options:

   Select File and Continue selects files containing the search string, then continues the search.

   Pause Search pauses after finding the search string within a file.
8. When the search string is found, and if the Pause Search option is turned on, choose one of the following:

   Next File searches the next file.

   Edit loads the hex editor with the cursor positioned at the first byte of the search string.

   Cancel ends the search and returns you to the active window.

See Also *Search Disk* and *Locate*

SELECT ALL TOGGLE

The Select All Toggle command selects or unselects all files in the active window.

To Select or Unselect All Files in the Active Window

1. Activate the file list from which you want to select or unselect all files.
2. Pull down the File menu.
3. Choose Select All Toggle.

Shortcut To unselect files quickly, press F4 or click Unsel on the message bar at the bottom of the PC Shell screen.

SET DATE/TIME

The Set Date/Time command allows you to set the date and time on your computer's clock.

To Set the Date and Time

1. Pull down the View menu.
2. Choose Set Date/Time.
3. Enter the new date in MM-DD-YY (month-date-year) format.
4. Enter the new time in HH:MM (hours:minutes) format.
5. Choose Set, or choose Cancel to return to PC Shell.

• **NOTE** In most computers the clock is battery-powered and needs to be set only once. If your computer doesn't have such a clock, and you want current date and time settings for your files, you must set the clock every time you turn on the machine.

See Also *Attribute Change*

SETTINGS

The Settings command on the Secure submenu sets options for encrypting and decrypting files.

To Change the Encryption and Decryption Settings

1. Pull down the **File** menu.
2. Choose **Secure**.
3. Choose **Settings**. The Secure Settings dialog box appears.
4. Choose from among the options (described in "Options").
5. Choose **OK** to save your changes, or choose **Cancel** to return to PC Shell.

• OPTIONS Choose from among the following options in the Secure Settings dialog box:

Full Encryption encrypts the file by using the complete Data Encryption Scheme (DES) algorithm (the most secure option).

Quick Encryption encrypts the file by using an abbreviated method (it runs twice as fast as a full encryption but is less secure).

No Encryption does not apply an encryption scheme to the file.

No Delete gives the encrypted file an .SEC extension. The original file is retained.

DOD Delete destroys the original file (Department of Defense method).

Quick Delete deletes files but does not overwrite them repeatedly. Files encrypted with this option are less secure, but the encryption is faster.

Compression reduces file sizes 25 percent to 60 percent. This option can be used during encryption with no perceptible loss of speed.

One Key allows you to encrypt a group of files with the same password. During encryption and decryption sessions, you are prompted only once for the password.

Expert Mode enables or disables the Master Key mode. When Expert Mode is selected, Master Key is disabled. This means the master key you created in your first PC Secure session cannot be used to decrypt the file if you lose the encryption password.

See Also *Decrypt File* and *Encrypt File; PC Secure* (Part 3)

SHOW INFORMATION

The Show Information command displays the following information about selected files: file name, extension, file path, file attributes, last time the file was accessed, file length, total clusters occupied, starting cluster number, and total files in directory.

To Display File Information

1. Select the file about which you want information.
2. Pull down the **O**ptions menu.
3. Choose **S**how Information.
4. Choose **OK** to return to PC Shell.

See Also *File Map*

SINGLE FILE LIST

The Single File List command displays a single set of Tree and File List windows. This command closes the second file list, the program list, and the View window.

To Display a Single File List

1. Pull down the **V**iew menu.
2. Choose **S**ingle File List.

See Also *Dual File Lists* and *Program/File Lists*

SORT FILES IN DIRECTORY

The Sort Files In Directory command sorts the files in a selected directory according to name, extension, size, date/time of creation, or selection order. You can also specify an ascending or a descending sort order.

To Sort the Files in a Directory

1. Select the directory whose files you want to sort.
2. Pull down the **D**isk menu.
3. Choose Sort Files In Directory. The Directory Sort dialog box appears.
4. Choose a Sort Field option and a Sort Method option.
5. Choose **S**ort to proceed, or choose **C**ancel to return to PC Shell.

6. Choose one of the following options:

   View sorts the directory without saving. Press any key or click the left mouse button to return to the dialog box.

   Update saves your changes and returns you to PC Shell.

   Cancel ends the sort and returns you to PC Shell.

   Resort returns you to the Directory Sort dialog box (see step 4).

• NOTES To view sorted subdirectories, choose the Refresh command from the View menu to reread the directory tree.

The File Display Options command gives you additional capabilities for sorting and displaying file lists.

See Also *File Display Options* and *Refresh*

SYSTEM INFO

The System Info command displays important information about your system's configuration. (It calls up the System Information utility.) You can view a summary screen or detailed screens about your system's configuration files, peripheral devices, disk-drive specifications, memory allocation, and overall system performance.

To Display Information about Your System's Configuration

1. Pull down the Special menu.
2. Choose **S**ystem Info.
3. Display additional detailed information as desired.
4. To exit, choose Exit on the message bar (F3), or pull down the **F**ile menu and choose Exit. Choose **O**K to confirm exiting.

To Obtain Detailed System Information

The System Information screen displays a summary of your system's configuration. There are several ways to open the detail windows:

- Press Enter repeatedly to see each detail window in order.
- Press the highlighted letter to obtain specific information about an item in a panel or menu. For example, pressing V for Video Adapter brings up detailed information about your system's video display, such as type, mode, character height, and more.
- Move the highlight to the desired item on the summary screen and press Enter.
- Using the mouse, click on any item.
- Use the pull-down menu commands.
- Use the function keys listed in the message bar at the bottom of the screen.

• NOTES The System Information screen contains three main windows of summary information about your system's configuration. Each window presents options for displaying detail screens. The three summary windows provide the following information:

Computer provides information about system type, operating system, and hardware setup.

Relative Performance provides information about the performance of your system's CPU and disk drives, and lets you compare the performance of your system with typical benchmark systems.

Memory displays the amounts and allocation schemes for conventional, extended, and expanded memory in your system. You can also display information on hardware and software interrupts.

See Also *System Information* (Part 3)

UNDELETE

The Undelete command locates and recovers accidentally deleted files and directories. Deleted files are displayed and rated for their potential for recovery. You can then recover them automatically or manually.

To Start Undelete

1. Pull down the **F**ile menu.
2. Choose **U**ndelete.

The Undelete screen appears, with a directory tree, a file list, and a Deleted File Status window. There are several ways to undelete files. Files that have been deleted are shown in the file list, and their status is shown in the Deleted File Status window.

To Undelete Files Using the Automatic Method

If the file status is listed as Perfect, Excellent, or Good, use the automatic method for undeleting files:

1. In the directory tree, select the directory from which you want to undelete files.
2. In the file list, select one or more files for undeleting.
3. Choose an option:

   - Press F8, or pull down the **F**ile menu and choose **U**ndelete. The undeleted file is recovered in its original location on the disk.
   - To write the recovered file to another disk, pull down the **F**ile menu and choose Undelete **T**o. Specify the target drive in the Drive Selection dialog box.

To Find Deleted Files

If the deleted file you want is not in the file list, you can search for it beyond the current directory by entering file specifications or by entering text strings contained within the files. You can also search for files associated with specific groups.

1. Pull down the **File** menu. The Find Deleted Files dialog box appears.
2. Choose **Find** Deleted Files.
3. Enter the file name and extension for the search.
4. Choose any of the following options:

   Containing sets up a specific character string as a search target.

   Ignore Case locates strings regardless of capitalization.

   Whole Word Search locates strings that occur as whole words only.

   Groups searches for deleted files associated with specific groups.

   Delete Sentry locates files deleted in Delete Sentry mode.

   Delete Tracker locates files deleted in Delete Tracker mode.

   DOS locates files deleted with the DEL command in DOS and with no data protection scheme.
5. Choose **OK** to proceed, or choose **Cancel** to return to the Undelete screen.

• NOTES PC Tools provides two data protection schemes: Delete Sentry and Delete Tracker, which greatly improve your chances of recovering deleted files. Delete Sentry copies all deleted files to a directory named SENTRY. It provides the greatest chances of recovery. Delete Tracker saves deleted file information in a file named PCTRACKR.DEL in your root directory. A file can be recovered if it has not been overwritten. Both protection schemes are available through the Data Monitor utility.

See Also *Undelete* (Part 3)

UNSELECT FILES

The Unselect Files command unselects files individually.

To Unselect Files in the File List

1. Pull down the View menu.
2. Choose **Unselect** Files. All selected files are no longer highlighted.

Shortcut To unselect files quickly, press F4 or click Unsel on the message bar at the bottom of the PC Shell screen.

VERIFY DISK

The Verify command on the Disk menu determines the integrity, or readability, of a disk. Verify Disk scans the entire disk, including files, directories, deleted files and unused space. If bad sectors are found, you can load the hex editor and repair them.

To Verify the Integrity of a Disk

1. Activate the drive you want to verify.
2. Pull down the **Disk** menu.
3. Choose **Verify**. The Disk Verify dialog box appears.
4. Choose **Verify** to continue. Sector numbers change as each sector is read. A message tells you whether the drive has been verified successfully. If an error is found, choose View/**Edit** to repair the sector, or choose **Verify** to continue verifying the disk.

See Also *Hex Edit File* and *Verify File*

VERIFY FILE

The Verify command on the File menu determines the integrity of data within selected files by scanning the files for bad sectors. Once the bad sectors are located, you can load the hex editor to repair them.

To Verify the Integrity of Files

1. Select one or more files you want to verify.
2. Pull down the File menu.
3. Choose Verify. The File Verify message window appears. Sector numbers change as each sector is read.
   - If the file is verified successfully, a message tells you the file is OK. The next file is then verified automatically.
   - If an error is found, choose View/Edit to repair the sector, or choose Verify to continue verifying files.

See Also *Hex Edit File* and *Verify Disk*

VERSION 6 MENUS

The Version 6 Menus command changes the structure of the pull-down menus to a format similar to that of PC Tools version 6. Turning on this option still gives you access to commands new to version 7.

To Change the Menu Format to Version 6

1. Pull down the Options menu.
2. Choose Version 6 Menus.

A check mark next to the Version 6 Menus command indicates that this option is turned on. No check mark indicates that version 7 menus are in effect.

VIEW/EDIT

The View/Edit command allows you to view and edit the contents of any sector on a disk, even if the sector is unused or contains data from a deleted file.

To View and Edit Disk Sectors

1. Select the drive you want to view or edit.
2. Pull down the **D**isk menu.
3. Choose View/**E**dit. The Disk Edit screen appears.
4. To edit the sector, press F7 or click Edit on the message bar at the bottom of the screen.
5. To save your changes, press F5 or click Save on the message bar.
6. To exit, press F3 or click Exit on the message bar.

• OPTIONS You are given the following options on the message bar of the Disk Edit screen:

F1 (Help)	Displays context-sensitive help screens
F2 (Index)	Displays an index of help topics
F3 (Exit)	Quits the current screen
F6 (Sector)	Allows you to change the viewed sector
F7 (Edit)	Allows you to edit the currently viewed sector
F8 (Name)	Displays the name, if any, of the file to which the sector is allocated

VIEW FILE CONTENTS

The View File Contents command displays the contents of selected files. You can view ASCII files, binary files, and document files created by application programs. Files created by most popular programs are displayed properly formatted.

To View the Contents of Selected Files

1. Select one or more files you want to view.
2. Pull down the **File** menu.
3. Choose **View File Contents**.

• **OPTIONS** Once the View window is activated, you can move around the file the way you would in most programs, using arrow keys, scroll bars, Page Up, Page Down, and so on. You still have access to all PC Shell pull-down menus and commands. In addition, the message bar at the bottom of the screen changes to give you access to the following function-key commands:

F1 (Help)	Displays context-sensitive help screens
F2 (Info)	Displays information about the viewed file
F3 (Exit)	Closes the View window
F4 (Launch)	Runs the program, if any, associated with the file
F5 (GoTo)	Allows you to specify a line, cell, or record number to move to in the viewed file
F6 (Viewer)	Displays a list of viewer formats you can use to view the current file
F7 (Search)	Searches the viewed file for the text string you specify

F8 (Unzoom/Zoom)	Shrinks and expands the View window
F9 (PrvFle)	Views the previously selected file
F10 (NxtFle)	Views the next selected file

See Also *Edit File* and *Hex Edit File*

VIEWER/FILE LISTS

The Viewer/File Lists command sets the configuration of PC Shell to include a directory tree, file list, and View window. As you select files, their contents are automatically displayed in the View window.

To Set the Viewer/File Lists Configuration

1. Pull down the **View** menu.
2. Choose **Viewer/File Lists**.

To turn off the Viewer/File Lists configuration, choose one of the following commands from the View menu: Single File List or Program/File Lists.

WAIT ON DOS SCREEN

The Wait On DOS Screen command is a toggle command that displays the message "Press any key or a mouse button to re-enter PC Shell" before you reenter PC Shell after running a command from the DOS command line.

To Toggle the Wait On DOS Screen Message

1. Pull down the **O**ptions menu.
2. Choose **W**ait On DOS Screen.

A check mark appears next to the Wait On DOS Screen command when it is turned on.

See Also *Overview: Running Applications from PC Shell*

Part Two

Desktop Manager

The Desktop Manager contains programs for organizing your data, taking notes, generating outlines, scheduling appointments, communicating with remote computers, and performing calculations. This part of the book begins with a brief discussion of the various ways you can start the Desktop Manager, then presents the Desktop utilities, organized alphabetically. Because these utilities are also standalone applications, each is broken down and its commands organized according to how you might logically use them. For example, the entry for the Notepads utility, a word processor, begins by explaining loading files, then editing text, and finishes with printing files.

OVERVIEW

This section explains the various ways you can start the Desktop Manager after you have installed it and how to remove it from memory.

STARTING THE DESKTOP MANAGER AS A STANDALONE APPLICATION

You can start the Desktop Manager from the DOS prompt just as you would any DOS application. Loading the Desktop Manager this way doesn't tie up any memory when you're not using it.

To Start the Desktop at the DOS Prompt

1. At the DOS prompt, type

   DESKTOP

2. Press Enter.

STARTING THE DESKTOP MANAGER AS A MEMORY-RESIDENT APPLICATION

Running the Desktop Manager in memory-resident mode enables you to use quick keystroke combinations, or *hotkeys*, to enter and quit the Desktop Manager while running other applications. When this mode is turned on, the Desktop Manager stays in memory while other applications are run. Switching between the Desktop Manager and your applications is quicker, but your applications may run more slowly.

Running the Desktop Manager in memory-resident mode gives you other advantages, including the following:

- You can run macros created using the Desktop Manager while you are in other programs.

- You can set alarms with the Appointment Scheduler to remind you of important events, even while you are in other programs.
- You can use the Clipboard to cut and paste text into other applications.
- You can send and receive electronic mail without leaving the program you're using.

• NOTES As a general rule, you need a minimum of 390K free memory to run the Desktop as a memory-resident program (the memory occupied by Desktop is not available to other programs). You may need to experiment to determine whether running Desktop in this mode is feasible on your machine. If your other programs run out of memory while Desktop is resident, remove the Desktop to provide more memory for those programs. On systems with at least 1MB RAM, you should be able to run Desktop in memory-resident mode without memory conflicts.

If you load the Desktop Manager as a memory-resident program, then load other memory-resident programs, you must unload the other programs before you can unload the Desktop Manager from memory.

To Start the Desktop in Memory-Resident Mode

1. At the DOS prompt, type

   DESKTOP /R

2. Press Enter.

Press Ctrl-spacebar from any application or from the DOS prompt to start the Desktop Manager. Press Ctrl-spacebar again to exit the Desktop Manager and return to your previous application.

STARTING THE DESKTOP MANAGER EVERY TIME YOU BOOT YOUR COMPUTER

You can set up your system to run the Desktop Manager every time you boot your computer. To do this, install the Desktop Manager command line in your AUTOEXEC.BAT file. Use the standard DOS format:

DESKTOP *parameters*

• **OPTIONS** You can use command-line options, or *parameters*, to control the way the Desktop Manager is loaded into your computer. Type the parameters after the program name, either at the DOS prompt or in your AUTOEXEC.BAT file:

/CS clears the screen and displays calendars as a background (memory-resident mode only). When Desktop is run as standalone application, calendars are displayed automatically.

/C3 or **/C4** designates either COM3 or COM4 as the serial port to which your modem is connected. Because COM3 and COM4 aren't standard, this option must include the interrupt request (IRQ) level and port address designations. Use the format /C3=*IRQ,base port address.* Both IRQ level and port address designations are stated in hexadecimal notation (refer to your hardware manuals for more information).

/DQ enables and disables the Quick Load feature. When you press the hotkeys to load the Desktop Manager, memory used by the current program is saved in a disk file. To make the Desktop Manager load more quickly, enable this option. This option takes effect only when the hotkeys are used from the DOS prompt (no application programs running).

/MM loads the Desktop Manager with no application windows open. When you use hotkeys to exit the Desktop Manager, the program remembers which windows are open and opens the same windows the next time you run it. For example, suppose you have a Databases and a Notepads window open and you exit the program by using the hotkeys. The next time you load the program the same windows are opened unless you specified the /MM option at the DOS command line when you loaded Desktop.

/R loads the Desktop Manager as a memory-resident application.

/RA loads the Desktop Manager as a memory-resident application and automatically displays the current day's appointments and To-Do List from the Appointment Scheduler. If you use this option in your AUTOEXEC.BAT file, be sure to make the DESKTOP command the last in the file, because no command that follows it can be executed until you exit Desktop.

• **NOTE** The System Information utility may provide information about port addresses that you can use when using the /C3 and /C4 options.

See Also *System Information* (Part 3)

REMOVING THE DESKTOP FROM MEMORY

There are two ways to remove the Desktop Manager from memory when it is running in memory-resident mode. You can do it from the DOS prompt or from within the program itself.

To Unload the Desktop at the DOS Prompt

1. At the DOS prompt, type

   KILL

2. Press Enter.

Using this command also unloads PC Shell, Backtalk, and DeskConnect when they are memory-resident.

To Unload the Desktop from within the Program

1. Pull down the Desktop main menu.

2. Choose **U**tilities.
3. Choose **U**nload PCTOOLS Desktop.
4. Choose **U**nload again to confirm, or choose **C**ancel to return to the Desktop.

APPOINTMENT SCHEDULER

The Appointment Scheduler lets you use your computer to keep track of appointments and schedules, and to create daily to-do lists of important tasks. You can also use the Appointment Scheduler to set alarms to remind you of appointments or other events.

To Use the Appointment Scheduler

1. Pull down the **D**esktop main menu.
2. Choose **A**ppointment Scheduler. The Appointment Scheduler dialog box appears.
3. From the Files box, choose the file with which you want to work.
4. You can do any of the following:
   - Choose **L**oad to load the selected file.
   - Choose **N**ew to create a new file.
   - Choose **C**ancel to return to the Desktop.
   - Choose **D**elete to remove a file.

Shortcut Using the mouse, you can load a file from the Appointment Scheduler dialog box simply by double-clicking on the file name.

• NOTES When you have loaded a file, the Appointment Scheduler screen appears. This screen consists of the Monthly Calendars window, the Daily Scheduler window, and the To-Do List window. The day selected in the Monthly Calendars window determines the day shown in the Daily Scheduler and the To-Do List, and the week displayed in the Weekly Appointment Scheduler.

You can use the following methods for navigating this screen:

- To open or close a window, click its Close box or press its corresponding function key (see below).
- To choose a day from the Monthly Calendars, use the arrow keys or simply click on the day. If, using the arrow keys, you move beyond the current month, the calendar automatically scrolls to the next (or previous) month.
- You can change months on the Monthly Calendars by pressing the Page Up and Page Down keys. Press Ctrl-Page Up and Ctrl-Page Down to change years. Press Home to return to the current date.
- With the Daily Scheduler or To-Do List activated, use the ← and → keys to change days. Press Home to return to the current date.
- To select entries from the Daily Scheduler or To-Do List, use the ↑ and ↓ keys, or simply click the entry with the mouse. Press Page Up and Page Down or click on the scroll bars to move to other parts of the current window.

The Desktop main menu is also available in the Appointment Scheduler. In addition, you are given access to the following function-key commands from the message bar at the bottom of the screen:

F4 (Day)	Hides or displays the Daily Scheduler window
F5 (Week)	Hides or displays the Weekly Appointment Scheduler window
F6 (Month)	Hides or displays the Monthly Calendars window
F7 (To-Do)	Hides or displays the To-Do List window
F8 (Usage)	Hides or displays the Time Usage Chart window

To Make an Appointment

1. Activate the Monthly Calendars. Move the cursor to the date for which you want to make an appointment.
2. Select the Daily Scheduler window (it has the selected day of the week and date for its title). Move the highlight to the time for the appointment.
3. Pull down the **Appointment** menu.
4. Choose **Make**. The Make Appointment dialog box appears.
5. Enter information. Choose **Make** again to confirm.

Shortcut You can open the Make Appointment dialog box by using the mouse: Simply double-click on the time entry for which you want to make an appointment.

• OPTIONS In the Make Appointment dialog box, you are given the following data fields for describing appointments:

Description identifies the appointment (24 characters).

Start date sets the first date for the appointment.

End date sets the last date for the appointment.

Time sets the time of day for the appointment.

Duration designates the length of time the appointment requires.

Settings opens the Special Appointment Settings box. Use the When column to specify how often the appointment is scheduled (one day only, weekly, monthly, etc.). You can also set an alarm, attach a note, or designate a type of appointment.

To Set the Alarm

1. Make an appointment using the procedures described above.
2. In the Make Appointment dialog box, choose **Settings**.

3. From the Alarm column, choose one of the following:

   Alarm on time sets the alarm for the exact time of the appointment.

   5 min advance sets the alarm for 5 minutes before the appointment.

   10 min advance sets the alarm for 10 minutes before the appointment.

To Make To-Do List Entries

1. Activate the To-Do List window.
2. Move the cursor to a blank line and type your entry.
3. Press Enter. The New To-Do Entry dialog box appears (with text from step 2, if entered, in the Description field).
4. Specify options.
5. Choose **Make**.

• **OPTIONS** You are given the following data fields for describing To-Do List entries:

Description identifies the To-Do List entry.

Start date sets the first date the entry appears on the To-Do List. The default is the current date.

End date sets the last date the entry appears. If no end date is selected, the entry appears in the To-Do List until it is deleted.

Priority designates an order of importance for entries.

Attach note links the entry to a Notepads document.

Repeat each year sets the entry to appear each year according to specified start and end dates.

To Print Your Schedule

1. From the Appointment Scheduler screen, pull down the File menu.
2. Choose **Print**.

3. From the Print dialog box, specify a period for which you want to print a schedule.
4. Use the Device command button to specify the printer and the port to which you want to send the file.
5. Use the Layout command button to specify a format for your document.
6. Choose Print.

CALCULATORS

The Desktop Manager features four types of calculators:

Algebraic performs standard arithmetic functions.

Financial emulates the HP-12C calculator; calculates simple interest, compound interest, and annual percentage rates.

Programmers emulates the HP-16C calculator; performs programming-related functions.

Scientific emulates the HP-11C calculator; calculates logarithmic, trigonometric, and other scientific functions.

To Open a Calculator

1. Pull down the Desktop main menu.
2. Choose Calculators.
3. Choose the calculator you want to use: Algebraic, Financial, Programmers, or Scientific.

The Calculator window appears, consisting of keyboard and calculator displays. To make entries, use the numeric keypad or the number keys across the top of your keyboard, or click on the keys in the keyboard display.

• OPTIONS In addition to the standard Desktop Manager function-key commands, you are given the options shown in Table 2.1 for each calculator. To execute the commands, press the corresponding function key or, using the mouse, click on the command name on the message bar at the bottom of the screen.

Table II.1: Calculator Options

Key	Name	Action
Algebraic		
F4	Clear	Clears the calculator display or tape
F5	Erase	Erases the calculator tape
Financial		
F4	None	Clears all register displays
F5	Stack	Displays the stack registers
F6	Fin	Displays the financial registers
Programmers		
F4	Stack	Displays the stack registers
F6	Data	Displays the data registers
Scientific		
F4	None	Clears all register displays
F5	Stack	Displays the stack registers
F6	Data	Displays the data registers

• NOTES *Registers* store lists of numbers until you exit the Calculator utility, turn off your computer, or clear the registers. To view the contents of a register, use the function key or pull down the RegisterDisplay menu and select the appropriate command.

Stack registers store numbers, such as the intermediate results of complex addition, subtraction, multiplication, and division operations or numbers from other registers. Financial registers (financial calculator only) calculate mortgage payments, interest rates, interest accrued, and other financial values. Data registers store numbers. Data registers are numbered 0 through 9 and .0 through .9.

CLIPBOARD

The Clipboard utility gives you a temporary storage area for text. You can cut and paste using the Clipboard when in other Desktop utilities (such as Calculators, Notepads, and Outlines) or from DOS applications. You can also edit text in the Clipboard. To cut and paste from DOS applications using the Clipboard, run the Desktop in memory-resident mode.

To Open the Clipboard

1. Pull down the Desktop main menu.
2. Choose Clipboard. The Clipboard window appears.

To Copy Text Using Hotkeys

1. Press Ctrl-Del to copy text to the Clipboard. A block cursor appears in the center of the screen.
2. Position the block cursor at the beginning of the block you want to copy. Press Enter.
3. Move the cursor to the end of the block. The block is highlighted. Press Enter. Selected text is copied to the Clipboard.

Shortcut To use the mouse to select a block of text, position the cursor at the beginning of the block, and click and drag to the end of the block. Release the mouse button to copy the text to the Clipboard.

To Paste Text Using Hotkeys

1. Position the cursor at the location where you want to paste text from the Clipboard.

2. Press Ctrl-Ins.

The Clipboard is saved until you copy over it or restart your computer. Thus, you can paste the same text in multiple locations, if desired.

To Copy Text Using Menu Commands

1. Pull down the Desktop main menu.
2. Choose Clipboard.
3. Pull down the Copy/Paste menu.
4. Choose Copy To Clipboard. The Clipboard window disappears, and the screen from the underlying application (Desktop or DOS) is displayed. A block cursor appears in the center of the screen.
5. Position the block cursor at the beginning of the block you want to copy. Press Enter.
6. Move the cursor to the end of the block. The block is highlighted.
7. Press Enter. The selected text is copied to the Clipboard.

Shortcut To use the mouse to select a block of text, position the cursor at the beginning of the block. Click and drag to the end of the block. Release the mouse button to copy the text to the Clipboard.

To Paste Text Using Menu Commands

1. Pull down the Desktop main menu.
2. Choose Clipboard.
3. Pull down the Copy/Paste menu.
4. Choose Paste From Clipboard. The Clipboard window disappears. The Clipboard text is pasted in the underlying application (Desktop or DOS) at the cursor position.

• **EXAMPLE** Suppose you want a quick way to move a range of numbers from your spreadsheet program into your word processing program. You know that your word processor contains an Import feature, but you find it too cumbersome for a small section. With the Desktop Manager loaded in memory-resident mode, follow these steps to perform this operation using the Clipboard:

1. Load your spreadsheet program and the file containing the data you want to move.
2. Press Ctrl-Del. The block cursor appears in the center of your screen.
3. Move the cursor to the top-left corner of the data you want to move. Press Enter.
4. Move the cursor to the bottom-right corner of the data you want to move. The selected block is highlighted as the cursor moves. Press Enter.
5. Exit the spreadsheet program.
6. Load your word processor and the file to which you want to paste the selected data.
7. Position your cursor where you want to paste the data.
8. Press Ctrl-Ins. The selected block is written to the word processor file.

• **NOTE** The Clipboard window is similar to the Notepads window and contains many, but not all, of the same commands. See the Notepads section for procedures on editing, searching, and printing text from the Clipboard.

DATABASES

The Databases utility allows you to organize, store, and manipulate databases, such as telephone directories, address books, and checkbooks.

To Open Databases

1. Pull down the Desktop main menu.
2. Choose Databases. The Database Files dialog box appears.

To Load an Existing Database File

From the Database Files dialog box, do one of the following:

- Enter the file name and extension of the database you want to load.
- Activate the Files list box, select the database file you want to open, and choose Load.
- Using the mouse, double-click on the database file you want to open.

The Databases window appears. Use the arrow keys, Tab key, and Page Up and Page Down keys to browse through records. Use the Browse command from the File menu to display multiple records on a single screen.

To Create a New Database File

1. In the opening Database Files dialog box, enter a name for the new file.
2. Choose New. The new file is created with a .DBF extension, unless you specified another. The Field Editor dialog box appears. (If you choose New without entering a file name, the file is given the name WORK.DBF.)
3. In the dialog box, enter a name for the first field.
4. Select a field type: Character, Numeric, Logical, or Date (explained in "Options").
5. Enter a field size in the Size box, or click on the ↑ and ↓ buttons to increase or decrease the displayed value. For numeric fields, enter the number of characters displayed to the right of the decimal point by using the Decimal box. Keep in mind that the decimal point counts as one character.

6. Choose **A**dd to create the field. The field is created and all boxes are cleared. Repeat steps 3 through 5 to create the next field.
7. Repeat steps 3 through 6 until all fields have been created. Choose **S**ave to create the database file. The database file window appears, displaying fields you have created.

To enter data in fields, pull down the **F**ile menu, choose **M**odify Data, and enter data.

• OPTIONS There are four field types in the Field Editor dialog box. The characters making up each type consist of the following:

Character: Letters and numbers used for identification purposes only, special symbols, and ASCII graphics characters. A character field can consist of 70 characters maximum.

Numeric: Numbers used as values for computations, a decimal point, the minus sign (for negative numbers), and the plus sign (for positive numbers). A numeric field can consist of 19 characters maximum.

Logical: A single character that represents a true or false condition. Use T, t, y, or Y for true. Use F, f, N, or n for false.

Date: An eight-character field representing month, day, and year. Enter dates in the format YYYY/MM/DD, even though dates are displayed in the format MM/DD/YY. For example, to display 01/22/93, enter 19930122 in the date field.

To Edit an Existing Database File

1. With the database file window displayed, pull down the **F**ile menu.
2. Choose **M**odify Data.
3. Pull down the **E**dit Menu and choose **E**dit Fields. The Field Editor dialog box appears.
4. Make changes to the field attributes.
5. Choose the appropriate command button:

   Add adds a field.

Delete removes a field.

Next moves to the next field.

Prev moves to the previous field.

Save saves changes to the database file.

Cancel cancels changes and returns you to the database file window.

To Edit Records in an Existing Database File

1. Open the database file window from which you want to edit records.
2. Move the highlight to the record and field you want to edit.
3. Make changes to text and press Enter.

To Add a New Record

1. Pull down the Edit menu.
2. Choose Add New Record. A blank record appears at the top of the file.
3. Enter data in fields. Once data is entered, the record is placed in sort order in the database file.

To Delete a Record

1. Select the record you want to delete.
2. Pull down the Edit menu.
3. Choose Delete Record.

• **OPTIONS** With the database file window displayed, you can use the keys in Table 2.2 to move around the file.

Table II.2: Movement Keys in the Database File Window

Key	Action
Tab	Moves to next field
Shift-Tab	Moves to previous field
Home	Moves to beginning of field
End	Moves to end of field
↑ or F5	Moves highlight up one line
↓ or F6	Moves highlight down one line
←	Moves cursor left one character
→	Moves cursor right one character
Ctrl-←	Moves cursor left one word
Ctrl-→	Moves cursor right one word
Ctrl-Home or F4	Moves highlight to first record in file
Ctrl-End	Moves highlight to last record in file
Home, Home	Moves highlight to top of window
End, End	Moves highlight to bottom of window
Page Up	Scrolls file up one screen
Page Down	Scrolls file down one screen
Ctrl-Page Up	Scrolls up one line without moving cursor
Ctrl-Page Down	Scrolls down one line without moving cursor

To Sort Database Records

1. Open the database file you want to sort.
2. Pull down the Edit menu.
3. Choose **S**ort Database. The Sort Field Select dialog box appears.
4. Select a field to use as the sort key. Use the command buttons **N**ext and **P**rev to move to the next or previous record.

5. Choose **S**ort to sort the file, or choose **C**ancel to close the Sort Field Select dialog box and return to the database file window.

Use the Sort Database command to sort records using any field as a sort key. You may sort using only one field at a time. The Sort Database command works in both Edit and Browse modes, although the sort results can be viewed more easily in Browse.

To Search for Text in All Fields

1. Open the database file you want to search.
2. To search all fields, do one of the following:
   - Pull down the **S**earch menu. Choose **F**ind Text In All Fields.
   - Press F7.
   - Using the mouse, click on the Search command button on the message bar at the bottom of the screen.

   The Search All Fields dialog box appears.
3. In the Search Data text box, enter a text string you want to use as a search target.
4. Choose an option: Search all records, Search selected records, or Search from current record.
5. Choose **S**earch. The database file window is displayed with the highlight on the record and field in which the target string is found, if any.
6. To search for the next occurrence of the target string, press F7 or click on the Search command button from the message bar at the bottom of the screen. Choose **S**earch again from the dialog box.

To Search for Text in the Sort Field

1. Open the database file you want to search.
2. Pull down the **S**earch menu.

3. Choose Find Text In Sort Field. The Search Sort Field dialog box appears.
4. In the Search Data text box, enter a text string you want to use as a search target.
5. Choose an option: Search all records, Search selected records, or Search from current record.
6. Choose Search. The database file window is displayed with the highlight on the record and field in which the target string is found, if any.
7. To search for the next occurrence of the target string, press F7 or click on the Search command button from the message bar at the bottom of the screen. Choose Search again from the dialog box.

To Select Records

1. Open the database file from which you want to select records.
2. Pull down the Edit menu.
3. Choose Select Records. The Select Records dialog box appears.
4. Enter the field name.
5. Enter the selection criteria. Use ? as a wildcard. Specify ranges using periods (..) to separate high and low values. For example, using the zip code field and entering 90000..99999 selects all zip codes from 90000 to 99999.
6. Choose Select to filter and select records. The database file window appears. Only the records meeting your selection criteria are displayed.

Use the Select Records command to configure your display and when sorting or printing database files.

To Print a Database File

1. Open the database file you want to print. If you want to print only selected records, select them now.
2. Pull down the **File** menu.
3. Choose **Print**. If you are in Edit mode, the Print Selection dialog box appears. Choose an option: Print selected records, Print current record, or Print field names. The Print dialog box appears.
4. Choose options:

   Device: Specify a printer port (LPT1, LPT2, LPT3, COM1, COM2, or Disk file).

   Number of copies: Specify up to 99 copies to print.

   Line spacing: Specify up to 4 spaces between each line.

   Starting page #: Specify the page on which to begin printing.
5. Choose **Print** to send the file to the printer, or choose **Cancel** to cancel printing and return to the database file window.

HOTKEY SELECTION

The Hotkey Selection command changes the Desktop Manager's default hotkeys for entering and exiting the program, cutting and pasting to the Clipboard, and auto-dialing telephone numbers.

To Change Hotkeys

1. Pull down the **Desktop** menu.
2. Choose **Utilities**.
3. Choose **Hotkey Selection**.
4. Select the hotkey you want to change.

5. Press the key combination you want to use as the new hotkey.
6. Click the Close box or press Escape to save your changes and return to Desktop.

Tip Use the Macro Editor to create other hotkey combinations to perform complex or frequently used operations.

MACRO EDITOR

The Macro Editor allows you to create and edit macros. A macro is a recorded series of keystrokes that you can play back, or execute, by pressing a single keystroke combination.

When you play back a macro, the keystrokes you have saved are executed starting at the cursor location in the current application. You can run macros in any application if you run Desktop in memory-resident mode. If you run Desktop as a standard application, macros can be run only from the Desktop.

To Open the Macro Editor

1. Pull down the **D**esktop main menu.
2. Choose **M**acro Editor. The Macro Files dialog box appears.

To Create a New Macro

1. In the Macro Files dialog box, enter a name for the new macro.
2. Choose **N**ew. A Notepads window appears with the specified file name and a .PRO extension.
3. If you want to include a comment that describes the macro, type it and press Enter.

4. Position the cursor in the first column of a new line. Press Alt-+. The text string <begdef> is displayed, which designates the beginning of the macro definition.

5. Enter the keystroke or keystroke combination that will be used to activate the macro. Make sure it is enclosed by angle brackets. To use a key in conjunction with Ctrl or Alt, simply press the key combination and the brackets will be inserted automatically. For example, if you press Ctrl-J, <ctrlj> is displayed in the macro window.

6. Enter the keystrokes and commands that make up the macro.

7. Press Alt-– to end the definition; <enddef> is displayed in the macro window.

8. To save your changes, pull down the **F**ile menu and choose **S**ave.

To Edit a Macro File

1. From the Files box in the Macro Files dialog box, select the macro you want to edit.

2. Choose **L**oad. The macro file window is displayed.

3. Edit the file as desired.

4. To save your changes, pull down the **F**ile menu and choose **S**ave.

To Activate a Macro

1. Open the macro file containing the macros you want to activate.

2. Pull down the **F**ile menu.

3. Choose **M**acro Activation.

4. Select an activation option: Not active, Active when in PCTOOLS Desktop, Active when not in PCTOOLS Desktop, or Active everywhere.

5. Choose **O**K.

6. Save the file: Pull down the **File** menu and choose **Save**.

Macros must be activated before they can be played back. Activating a macro saves it in memory so that it is available to be run.

To Play Back a Macro

1. Place the cursor at the location from which you want to run the macro.
2. Press the keystroke sequence that plays back the macro. The macro plays back as created. (Press Escape to terminate a macro that is running.)

You can play back a macro from any PC Tools or DOS application, depending on whether Desktop is memory-resident and depending on the activation option you selected.

• **EXAMPLE** Suppose you write memos frequently and you want to create a macro that automatically inserts your memo heading in a file. Your heading consists of the words MEMO, TO, FROM, and RE along the left margin. All are separated by two line spaces. You decide to assign the keystroke combination Alt-M to your macro.

To create this macro, follow these steps:

1. With Desktop loaded memory-resident, pull down the **D**esktop menu.
2. Choose **M**acro Editor. The Macro Files dialog box appears.
3. Enter the file name MEMO.PRO. Choose **N**ew to create the new file.
4. Press Alt-+ to begin the macro definition.
5. Press Alt-M to designate this keystroke combination for your macro.
6. Type **MEMO:**. Then press F7-Enter, F7-Enter. (Pressing Enter alone inserts a line return in your macro file but does not record the keystroke in your macro. You must press F7 and Enter together so that a line return is inserted when you play back the macro.)

7. Type **TO:**. Then press F7-Enter, F7-Enter.
8. Type **FROM:**. Then press F7-Enter, F7-Enter.
9. Type **RE:**. Then press F7-Enter, F7-Enter.
10. Press Alt-- to end the macro definition. The macro should be displayed on the screen as

    <begdef><altm>MEMO:<enter><enter>TO:<enter><enter> FROM:<enter><enter>RE:<enter><enter><enddef>

11. Pull down the **F**ile menu. Choose **S**ave. The Save File To Disk dialog box appears. Choose **S**ave again.
12. To activate the macro, pull down the **F**ile menu and choose **M**acro Activation. To activate the macro so that you can run it in your word processor, choose either of the following: Active when not in PCTOOLS Desktop, or Active everywhere. Choose **OK**.
13. Exit the Desktop Manager.
14. Load your word processor and the file from which you want to run the macro.
15. Position the cursor where you want the memo heading to begin.
16. Press Alt-M.

• NOTES When Desktop is run memory-resident, keystroke combinations assigned to macros override the same keystroke combinations in applications. For example, suppose you create a macro activated by pressing Shift-F3, and your word processor uses Shift-F3 to switch between document windows. If the macro is activated, pressing Shift-F3 plays back the macro, even when you are in your word processor. Similarly, if you create macros using the Alt keys, you may override the pull-down menu commands in Desktop Manager and PC Shell. Use caution when assigning keystroke combinations to macros that you may need in other programs.

MODEM TELECOMMUNICATIONS

The Modem Telecommunications utility allows you to send and receive files between remote computers connected via telephone lines. It also allows you to dial and hang up calls, and to create, store, and edit a telephone directory that specifies connection protocols for remote terminals.

To Open Modem Telecommunications

1. Pull down the Desktop main menu.
2. Choose Telecommunications.
3. Choose Modem Telecommunications. The default telephone directory (PHONE.TEL) window is displayed.

To Create a Directory Entry

1. Pull down the Edit menu.
2. Choose Create New Entry. The Edit Phone Directory dialog box appears.
3. Enter data in fields as described in "Options."
4. Choose Next Screen. The second Edit Phone Directory dialog box appears.
5. Set telecommunications options to match those of the receiving terminal.
6. Choose OK to create the entry, or choose Cancel to return to the phone directory window.

To Edit a Directory Entry

1. Position the highlight at the entry you want to edit.
2. Pull down the Edit menu.

3. Choose **E**dit Entry. The Edit Phone Directory dialog box appears with information from the current entry in the fields.
4. Edit data in the fields.
5. Choose **N**ext Screen. The second Edit Phone Directory dialog box appears.
6. Edit telecommunications options, if desired.
7. Choose **OK** to save your changes, or choose **C**ancel to return to the phone directory window.

• OPTIONS The Edit Phone Directory dialog box contains the following fields and settings options you can use when creating and editing directory entries:

NAME identifies the person or company receiving the communications.

DATABASE sets the path and name of the database containing the fields of data to be sent.

FIELD 1 and **FIELD 2** designate fields within the specified database, to be used in conjunction with script files.

PHONE contains the phone number and any additional dialing commands.

SCRIPT identifies the script file (with the .SCR extension), which contains automated procedures.

USER ID is your personal access code, used to log on to communication services.

PASSWORD is a secret code used to restrict access to online communication services.

BAUD RATE sets the speed of transmission.

PARITY is usually the eighth bit in a data byte. The parity bit is used in error-checking schemes to ensure the integrity of the transmission. The most common settings are NONE and EVEN.

TERMINAL designates emulation modes and is usually used in network systems.

FLOW CONTROL controls the flow of data between two computers when XON/OFF is chosen.

EOL RECEIVE specifies how the sending computer marks the ends of lines in ASCII transfers.

EOL SEND specifies how your computer marks the ends of lines in ASCII transfers.

DATA BITS designates the number of actual data bits in a transmitted character, or byte. Most communication schemes use EIGHT.

STOP BITS specifies the number of bits (one or two) used to indicate the end of a character. Most communication schemes use ONE.

DUPLEX sets the transmission mode. Set to FULL, the modem can send and receive simultaneously. Set to HALF, the modem sends and receives, but not simultaneously. Most communication schemes use FULL.

To Dial a Number Automatically

1. In the phone directory window, select the directory entry you want to call.
2. Dial the number by doing one of the following:
   - Press F7.
   - Pull down the Actions menu and choose Dial.
   - Using the mouse, double-click on the directory entry.
3. When the connection is established, the Telecommunications window appears. If your directory entry includes a script file, it is executed. If not, enter commands and type responses to questions.

To Dial a Number Manually

1. Select an entry with the same telecommunications settings you want to use.
2. Dial the number by doing either of the following:
   - Press F8.
   - Pull down the Actions menu and choose Manual.

To Send a File with an ASCII Protocol

1. With the Telecommunications window open, press F4, or pull down the **Send** menu and choose **Send**.
2. Choose **ASCII**. The File Load dialog box appears.
3. Select the file you want to send. Choose **Load** to send the file.

To Send a File with an XMODEM Protocol

1. With the Telecommunications window open, press F5, or pull down the **Send** menu and choose **Send**.
2. Choose **XMODEM**. The File Load dialog box appears.
3. Select the file you want to send. Choose **Load** to send the file.

To Receive a File with an ASCII Protocol

1. Open the Save dialog box by pressing F6 or pulling down the **Receive** menu and choosing **ASCII**.
2. In the Filename text box, enter the path and name of the file you want to receive.
3. Choose **Save** to save the information sent to your screen, either by you or from a remote computer.
4. When the transfer is finished, pull down the **Actions** menu and choose **End Transfer**.

To Receive a File with an XMODEM Protocol

1. Open the Save dialog box by pressing F7 or pulling down the **Receive** menu and choosing **XMODEM**.

2. In the Filename text box, enter the path and name of the file you want to receive.
3. Choose Save to save the information sent to your screen, either by you or from a remote computer.
4. When the transfer is finished, pull down the Actions menu and choose End Transfer.

To Hang Up the Phone

1. Log off the remote computer.
2. Press F8, or pull down the Actions menu and choose Hangup Phone.

NOTEPADS

The Notepads utility allows you to create, edit, format, and print text documents of up to 60,000 characters (60K).

To Open Notepads

1. Pull down the Desktop main menu.
2. Choose Notepads. The Notepads dialog box appears.

To Create a Notepad File

1. From the Notepads dialog box, enter a new name for the file in the Filename text box.
2. Choose New. The file window appears with the name of the new file at the top.

To Load an Existing Notepad File

1. Open the Notepads dialog box.
2. To select a file to load, do either of the following:
   - In the Filename text box, enter the name of the file you want to load. Press Enter or choose Load.
   - Activate the Files box, and select the file you want to load. Press Enter or choose Load.

The selected Notepads file appears in the window.

• OPTIONS The Notepads utility provides the following function-key commands in addition to the standard Desktop function keys:

F4 (Load)	Opens the Notepads (file load) dialog box
F5 (Email)	Sends the current Notepads file as an electronic-mail message
F6 (Find)	Opens the Find And Replace dialog box
F7 (Again)	Locates the next occurrence of the target string specified in the Find And Replace dialog box
F8 (Spell)	Runs the Spellcheck utility for the current Notepads file

To Enter and Edit Text

1. Load the Notepads file you want to edit, or create a new file.
2. Enter and edit text as desired.

• OPTIONS Entering and editing text with Notepads is similar to doing so with most word processors. Use the commands shown in Table 2.3 to move the cursor and edit text.

Table II.3: Movement and Editing Keys in Notepads

Key	Action
Tab	Inserts a tab at the cursor position
↵	Inserts a hard return at the cursor position and starts a new line
Delete	Deletes the character above the cursor
Backspace	Deletes the character to the left of the cursor
↑	Moves up one line
↓	Moves down one line
→	Moves right one character
←	Moves left one character
Ctrl-→	Moves right one word
Ctrl-←	Moves left one word
Home	Moves the cursor to the beginning of the line
End	Moves the cursor to the end of the line
Ctrl-Home	Moves the cursor to the beginning of the file
Ctrl-End	Moves the cursor to the end of the file
Home, Home	Moves the cursor to the top of the window
End, End	Moves the cursor to the bottom of the window
Page Up	Scrolls up one window
Page Down	Scrolls down one window
Ctrl-Page Up	Scrolls text up one line without moving the cursor
Ctrl-Page Down	Scrolls text down one line without moving the cursor

To Save a Notepads File

1. Pull down the File menu.
2. Choose Save. The Save File To Disk dialog box appears. The name of the current file is displayed in the Filename text box.
3. Press Enter to accept the name of the current file. To save the file under a different name, enter the new name and press Enter.
4. Choose options:

   Make backup file saves an additional copy of the file with the same name and a .BAK extension.

   PCTOOLS Desktop saves the file in PCTOOLS Desktop format. Saving with this option retains formatting and control characters.

   ASCII saves the file in ASCII format. Saving with this option retains only text; formatting and control characters are removed.
5. Choose Save to save your changes, or choose Cancel to return to the file window without saving changes.

Warning When editing your AUTOEXEC.BAT or CONFIG.SYS file, always save it in ASCII format. Saving these files in PCTOOLS Desktop format may cause them not to run or to run improperly.

To Save Files Using Autosave

1. Pull down the File menu.
2. Choose Autosave. The Automatic File Save dialog box appears.
3. Set the interval for Autosave. Use the arrow keys or click on the scroll bar.
4. Choose ON to turn Autosave on.
5. Choose OK.

The Autosave command automatically saves Notepads files at specified intervals. This command provides an extra margin of safety against losing files because of power outages. Autosave is applied globally—it is turned on or off for all Notepads files.

To Mark a Block Using the Keyboard

1. Place the cursor at the beginning of the block of text you want to cut or copy.
2. Pull down the Edit menu.
3. Choose Mark Block.
4. Use the arrow keys to move the cursor to the end of the block. The block is highlighted.

To Mark a Block Using the Mouse

1. Click at the beginning of the text block.
2. While holding down the mouse button, move to the end of the text block. Release the mouse button. The block is highlighted.

To Cut, Copy, and Paste Text

1. Mark the block of text you want to cut or copy.
2. Pull down the Edit menu.
3. Choose Cut to Clipboard or Copy to Clipboard. The text block is either cut (the original text is deleted) or copied (the original text remains) to the Clipboard.
4. Move the cursor to the location at which you want to paste text from the Clipboard.
5. Pull down the Edit menu.
6. Choose Paste From Clipboard. The text is pasted at the current location.

You can use this procedure to cut or copy text from your Notepads file and paste it elsewhere in the same file, in another Notepads file, in another Notepads application, or in a DOS application (when Desktop is run in memory-resident mode).

Text copied to the Clipboard remains there until you cut or copy another text block to it, so you can paste the same text in multiple locations.

To Find Text

1. Pull down the **S**earch menu.
2. Choose **F**ind. The Find dialog box appears.
3. Enter the target string in the Search For text box (44 characters maximum).
4. Choose options:

   Case sensitive specifies that characters and capitalization must match exactly.

   Whole words only finds character strings only as complete words. For example, if searching for *form,* Notepads finds *form* but not *format* when this option is turned on.
5. Choose **F**ind. Notepads searches the file for the target string. If the string is located, the dialog box disappears and the cursor is positioned at the first occurrence of the string.
6. To find the next occurrence of the target string, if any, pull down the **S**earch menu and choose Find **A**gain.

To Replace Text

1. Pull down the **S**earch menu.
2. Choose **R**eplace. The Find And Replace dialog box appears.
3. In the Search For text box, enter the character string to be used as the search target.
4. In the Replace With text box, enter the character string to be used to replace the target string.
5. Choose options:

   Replace one time finds the first occurrence of the target string and replaces it.

Replace all finds and replaces all occurrences of the target string.

Verify before replace finds each occurrence of the target string and replaces the string only if you press Enter. It also gives you options to press Escape to cancel or spacebar to skip an occurrence.

Case sensitive finds strings in which characters and capitalization match exactly.

Whole words only finds character strings only as complete words. For example, if searching for *form,* Notepads finds *form* but not *format* when this option is turned on.

6. Choose Replace to execute the command according to the specified options, or choose Find to locate the target string without making changes.

To Insert a File

1. Place the cursor at the location in the current file where you want to insert a file.
2. Pull down the Edit menu.
3. Choose Insert File. The Notepads dialog box appears.
4. Enter the name of the file you want to insert, or select the file from the Files list box.
5. Choose Load. The selected file is added to the current file at the cursor position.

To Check Spelling in a File

1. Pull down the Edit menu.
2. Choose one of the Spellcheck commands:

   Spellcheck Word checks the spelling of the selected word

   Spellcheck Screen checks the spelling of all the text on the current screen.

   Spellcheck File checks the spelling of all text in the file.

3. Spellcheck compares the spelling of text in the file to an internal dictionary. If there are discrepancies, the Word Misspelled dialog box appears. Choose an option:

   Ignore skips the occurrence of the word's spelling and and further occurrences in the file.

   Correct displays the Word Correction dialog box with suggested correct spellings. Select the correct spelling or enter the correct spelling in the top box. Choose Accept or Cancel.

   Add saves the spelling of the current word to the internal dictionary and continues.

   Quit cancels Spellcheck and returns you to the file window.

4. Repeat step 2 until the entire selection or file has been checked.

To Format Pages for Printing

1. Pull down the Controls menu.
2. Choose Page Layout. The Page Layout dialog box appears.
3. Choose options. Enter values in the appropriate boxes, use the arrow keys to increase and decrease values, or click on the ↑ and ↓ symbols.

   Left margin sets the number of spaces between the left edge of the paper and the first printed character.

   Right margin sets the number of spaces between the right edge of the paper and the end of the printed line.

   Paper width specifies the width of the paper. For example, if you are using 8.5" × 11" paper and your printer is set for 10 characters per inch, use 85 as your paper width.

   Top margin sets the number of blank lines between the top of the page and the first printed line. To leave enough room for headers, this value should be no less than 2.

   Bottom margin sets the number of blank lines between the bottom of the page and the last printed line. To leave enough room for footers, this value should be no less than 2.

Paper size specifies the length of the paper, in lines. For example, if you are using 8.5" × 11" paper and your printer is set for 6 lines per inch, 66 is your paper size.

4. Choose **OK** to accept changes, or choose **Cancel** to cancel changes and return to the file window.

To Insert Headers and Footers

1. Pull down the **Controls** menu.
2. Choose **Header/Footer**. The Page Header & Footer dialog box appears.
3. Enter text in the Header text box (up to 50 characters).
4. Enter text in the Footer text box (up to 50 characters).
5. Choose **OK** to save the header and footer as displayed, or choose **Cancel** to cancel the operation and return to the file window.

Tip You can use the pound character (#) in headers or footers to automatically insert page numbers.

To Print a Notepads File

1. Pull down the **File** menu.
2. Choose **Print**. The Print dialog box appears.
3. Choose a Device option:

   LPT1, LPT2, or **LPT3** designates a parallel port for the printer.

   COM1 or **COM2** designates a serial port for the printer.

   Disk file writes the file to a disk file, using specified formatting, headers, and footers. The disk file is given the same name with a .PRT extension.
4. Specify the number of copies, the line spacing, and the starting page number. Enter values in the appropriate boxes, use the arrow keys to increase and decrease values, or click on the ↑ and ↓ symbols.

5. Choose Print, or choose Cancel to cancel printing and return to the file window.

To Save Setup Options

1. Pull down the Controls menu.
2. Choose Save Setup.

The Save Setup command saves the printing and formatting settings from the current file as the default for all files in the Notepads, Outlines, and Databases utilities.

To Exit Notepads without Saving the File

1. Pull down the File menu.
2. Choose Exit Without Saving.

OUTLINES

The Outlines utility allows you to create lists of topics and ideas organized in standard outline format. You can organize documents according to headlines and subheadlines. Each headline level represents a level of greater detail. You can view higher levels of your outline to get an overview of your document, or you can expand levels to get a detailed view.

To Enter Headlines

1. Press Tab to move the cursor to the headline level you want.
2. Enter headline text, and press Enter. The cursor moves to the same headline level on the next line.

To Change Headline Levels

1. Position the cursor at the beginning of the headline.
2. To promote a headline to a higher level, press Backspace, or pull down the Headlines menu and choose Promote.
3. To demote a headline to a lower level, press Tab, or pull down the Headlines menu and choose Demote.

To Collapse Headlines

1. Pull down the Headlines menu.
2. Choose Collapse Current. Subheadlines of the current headline are hidden, and an arrowhead symbol appears to the left of the current headline, indicating hidden levels.

To Show Only the Main Headlines

1. From anywhere in the document, pull down the File menu.
2. Choose Main Headline Only. All headlines except those on the first level are collapsed. The arrowhead symbol appears to the left of all headlines with hidden subheadlines.

To Expand Headlines

1. Position the cursor on the headline you want to expand (to display hidden subheadlines and text).
2. Pull down the Headlines menu.
3. Choose Expand Current to expand only the current level, or choose Expand All to expand all levels for all headlines.

To Show One Level of Headlines

1. Position the cursor in a headline at the level you want to display.
2. Pull down the Headlines menu.

3. Choose Show Level. All headlines below the level of the current headline are hidden.

• **NOTE** The Outlines utility uses many of the same command routines as the Notepads utility. To open the Outlines utility, create new files, load existing files, find and replace text, save files, or print files, follow the procedures described in the Notepads section.

Part Three

Data Recovery and System Utilities

This part of the book covers all of PC Tools' data recovery and system utilities, including the Windows utilities. They are presented in alphabetical order.

Advanced users can benefit from sections titled "Running from DOS or a Batch File." These sections provide command-line formats and options that can be used to configure and run PC Tools utilities automatically (bypassing menus and dialog boxes).

BACKTALK

The Backtalk utility enables background communications. You can set up a file transfer, then go to another application while the transfer continues unattended. It is a memory-resident utility that occupies roughly 64K of resident memory. It must be loaded before the Desktop Manager (the Desktop must be loaded as a memory-resident program as well).

To Load Backtalk from DOS or a Batch File

Enter the following command at the DOS prompt, or add it to your AUTOEXEC.BAT file. Use *n* to represent the serial port for which your modem is configured.

BACKTALK /*n*

• OPTIONS Use the following slash (/) commands to configure Backtalk for serial ports COM1 through COM4:

/1	Configures Backtalk for COM1
/2	Configures Backtalk for COM2
/C3 = *IRQ,base port address*	Configures Backtalk for COM3
/C4 = *IRQ,base port address*	Configures Backtalk for COM4

If you use either COM3 or COM4, you must include, in hexadecimal notation, the interrupt request level and port address designations. For example, you might use the command line

BACKTALK /3=4,3E8

Refer to your hardware manuals for specific information on interrupt request and port address designations.

Tip To add a Backtalk command to your AUTOEXEC.BAT file automatically, use the PC Tools Install program. Simply enable the Load Backtalk option in the Desktop Manager Configuration dialog box.

To Transfer Files in Background Mode

1. Load Backtalk and start Desktop in memory-resident mode.
2. Establish the connection with PC Tools Modem Telecommunications, and start the file transfer.
3. Press Alt-B to enter background mode. The program returns to the Desktop Manager.

You now can work run Desktop applications, or exit the Desktop and run DOS programs. The file transfer continues without further input. A blinking *B* in the upper-right corner of your screen indicates the background operation. A beep signals completion of the transfer.

• NOTES When you transfer files in background mode with the XMODEM protocol or with a BACKTALK command in your script file, a log file is created that summarizes the transfer operation. The TRANSFER.LOG file tells you whether your transfer has been successful. The first line of this file contains the name of the file transferred. The last line contains the word *Completed.* If problems occur, the last line contains error messages, such as "Time Out," "CRC Error," or "Too Many Retries."

Warning When transferring files in background mode, do not select the background COM port for any foreground operation. This conflict interrupts the file transfer.

See Also *Modem Telecommunications* (Part 2)

COMMUTE

The Commute utility allows one computer to take control of another. For example, you can use Commute to operate your desktop machine from a remote location with your laptop. Using your laptop you can transfer files, run programs, and make backups on your desktop machine.

To run Commute, you must first establish a connection: by network, by modem, or by direct connection using a null modem cable. One computer loads Commute as a memory-resident program and waits for a call. The other computer can then call the first computer and take (or give) control. Once control is established, you can use the Session Manager to perform operations such as chatting with the other operator and transferring files.

To Load Commute

1. At the DOS prompt, enter the command

   COMMUTE

   The program is loaded. The first time you run Commute, you are prompted to enter a user name, the type of connection you want as the default, and, if you select Modem Connection, the configuration of your modem. Then the Call Manager window appears.

2. Choose from these options:

   Call and Take Control displays the Private Call List dialog box. This option allows you to edit the call list, then call and take control of another computer on the list.

   Call and Give Control displays the Give Control List dialog box. This option allows you to edit the list of callers authorized to take control of your machine. You can then call and give control of your computer to one of the users on the list.

   Wait for Any Caller loads Commute as a memory-resident program in Wait mode. With this option on, your computer accepts calls from any Commute user.

   Wait from Call List loads Commute as a memory-resident program in Wait mode and accepts calls from any user on the appropriate call list.

   Wait for One Caller loads Commute as a memory-resident program and accepts calls from a single user that you specify.

To Wait for a Call

1. Choose Wait For Any Caller, Wait From Call List, or Wait For One Caller from the Call Manager window.
2. The next step is dependent on your choice in step 1:
   - If you chose Any Caller or Call List, the Connection-Type dialog box appears. Change the connection type, as needed. Then choose **OK** to continue.
   - If you chose One Caller, the Give Control List dialog box appears. Select the remote users to which you are giving control of your machine. Then choose **OK** to continue.

The program is loaded, and you are returned to DOS. You can now continue working on your machine. A dialog box appears when a caller is detected. When control is taken, the scroll light on your keyboard blinks repeatedly.

To Take Control of a Remote Machine

1. From the Call Manager window, choose Call And Take Control. The Private Call List dialog box appears.
2. Select the remote user you want to call and take control. Then choose **OK** to continue.

Commute calls the remote machine. A dialog box displays the progress of the connection process. When a connection is established, your computer displays whatever is on the remote machine's screen.

To Load the Session Manager

1. Once you have control of another machine, press the Session Manager hotkey (the default is Alt-Right Shift). The Session Manager is loaded.
2. Choose from these options:

   End the Session ends the Commute program and breaks the connection.

   Look at Your PC returns your machine to DOS. Use this option to check file names, make room on your disk for file transfers, or perform other DOS tasks. Type *EXIT* at the DOS prompt to return to the Session Manager.

Chat with Other PC opens the Chat window and lets you and the remote user enter comments interactively. With this window open, press F10 to ring a bell to alert the remote user.

Send Files to Other PC copies a file or group of files to the remote machine.

Get Files from Other PC copies a file or group of files from the remote machine.

Advanced Options opens the Advanced Options dialog box.

To Send Files Using the Session Manager

1. From the Session Manager window, choose Send Files To Other PC. The Send Files To Other PC dialog box appears.
2. Enter the path and name of the file you want to send in the appropriate field. Use DOS wildcards (* and ?) to specify groups of files. Use the minus sign (–) to exclude groups of files.
3. Enter a directory path to which you want to copy the files you send.
4. Select file transfer options as desired:

   Compress Files compresses files *in memory* before they are sent. Files are decompressed before they are copied to their destination directory. Use this option to speed up file transfers (the default setting is On).

   Automatic Overwrite allows you to overwrite files in the destination directory. When this option is off, a confirmation dialog box appears if you attempt to overwrite an existing file.

   Disable Virus Checking scans sent files for viruses. If a virus is detected, a confirmation dialog box appears allowing you to cancel the transfer.

   Include Subdirectories transfers files in any subdirectory of the current directory that meet the file specification.

Copy Only If Archive Bit Set transfers only files that have their archive attributes set. Use this option when running backups from a remote machine.

Clear Archive Bit After Copy clears archive bits on sent files.

Copy Newer Files Only overwrites existing files in the destination directory only when the sent files have been modified (as indicated by their date/time attributes) more recently. Use this option if you don't want to overwrite newer files on the destination directory.

5. When you have selected the options you want, choose **OK** to send the files.

To Receive Files Using the Session Manager

1. From the Session Manager window, choose Get **F**iles From Other PC. The Get Files From Other PC dialog box appears.
2. Enter the path and name of the files you want to receive from the remote computer. Use DOS wildcards (* and ?) to specify groups of files. Use the minus sign (–) to exclude groups of files.
3. Enter a path to which you want to copy received files.
4. Select file transfer options as desired (see the section above, "To Send Files Using The Session Manager").
5. Choose **OK** to receive files.

• **OPTIONS** The options that follow are available by choosing Advanced Options from the Session Manager window:

Reboot Other PC reboots the computer you are controlling. Your own computer is unaffected.

Lock Other Keyboard prevents keyboard input on the remote machine. This option works only if the remote machine has not turned off the Allow Other PC To Lock Your Keyboard option from the Security Settings menu.

Print Direction designates which printer or printers are used. You can choose your printer, the remote printer, both printers, or neither printer.

Redraw Your Screen refreshes your screen display. Use this command if you see incorrect characters on your screen. These usually are caused by line interference.

Save Current Screen saves a text file of the screen display. This option does not work with graphics screens.

Screen Options displays the Screen Options dialog box. This option allows you to select screen resolution, refresh rate, and EGA/VGA colors.

Keyboard Level resolves keyboard conflicts. Use this option if your keyboard does not work when controlling another machine.

● **NOTE** When you take control of another computer, your screen and the remote computer's screen show the same displays. Your keyboard and mouse commands control the remote computer's programs, disk drives, and printers. When you give control, the remote user operates your machine.

COMMSML

The COMMSML utility is a version of Commute that uses less conventional memory when run as a memory-resident program. Use this utility if you want to wait for a call, but cannot afford to tie up large areas of memory. When a call is answered, more memory is required. Once the call is completed, however, the smaller portion is used again.

To Wait for a Call with COMMSML

1. At the DOS prompt, enter the command

   COMMSML

   The Call Manager window appears.
2. Choose Wait For Any Call.

Shortcut To skip step 2, enter **COMMSML /R** at the DOS prompt.

COMPRESS

The Compress utility optimizes your hard disk by rearranging fragmented disk files into contiguous sectors and moving all free space to the end of the disk. This increases disk-access speeds and improves the chances of data recovery.

Compress analyzes your disk and recommends a compression technique. You can choose to use the recommended technique or perform a compression according to your own specifications.

Compress also gives you options for

- Moving directories and files to the beginning of the disk for quicker access
- Arranging files within directories in specified orders
- Specifying files, such as copy-protected or hidden files, that are not moved during the compression
- Wiping data from unused parts of the disk
- Showing files contained in a block
- Analyzing disk fragmentation

Warning Do not run Compress if there are deleted files on the disk you might want to recover. Compress writes over unused and unallocated sections of your disk; deleted files are almost always overwritten. To recover deleted files, run Undelete first.

Also, remove all memory-resident programs that might access the disk during the compression operation, including disk-caching programs other than PC-Cache.

To Load Compress at the DOS Prompt

At the DOS prompt, enter

COMPRESS

To Optimize Your Hard Disk Using the Recommended Compression

1. Load Compress. A message window appears as the file allocation table (FAT) is read, directories and files are processed, directory and file chains are tracked, and a compression technique is recommended. To proceed with the recommended compression, choose Compress.
2. A warning appears instructing you to remove memory-resident programs and to back up your disk before running Compress.
    - If you need to remove memory-resident programs or back up your disk, choose Cancel to return to the Compress screen, then press F3 to return to DOS.
    - To proceed with the compression, choose Compress again. Then choose OK to confirm.
3. When the compression ends, a dialog box appears with the following options:
    - Choose Mirror to save Mirror information.
    - Choose Exit to return to the DOS prompt.
    - Choose Continue to return to the Compress screen.

To Compress a Disk Using Specified Options

1. Load Compress. The Compress screen appears.
2. Pull down the Options menu.
3. Choose Compression Technique. A new dialog box appears.

4. Choose one of the following compression techniques:

   Optimize Directories moves directories to the front of the disk for faster access but does not move or unfragment files. Free space is not consolidated. Use this option if you have added or removed directories.

   Optimize Free Space consolidates free space but does not unfragment files. Use this option when you need a large area of free space, such as when copying large files or groups of files.

   Unfragment Files optimizes files but does not move directories or consolidate free space. Use this option often to prevent new files from becoming unacceptably fragmented.

   Full Optimization unfragments files, arranges files and directories according to selections from the Options menu, and consolidates free space. Use this option monthly to completely optimize your disk. It is the slowest option, but it provides the greatest performance increase.

   Full Optimization With Clear performs a full optimization and wipes all data in unused sectors. Before using this option, recover any data you might need.

   File Sort only rearranges the files according to selections from the Options menu (no compression occurs).

5. You can now specify further options (see the procedures discussed in "To Choose an Ordering Method" and "To Analyze Your Disk for Optimization").

6. If desired, you can generate a report of compression activities. The report details cluster allocation, options selected, and time required. Pull down the **O**ptions menu and choose **P**rint Report. Then choose **P**rinter or **D**isk as the destination for your report.

7. Pull down the **C**ompress menu.

8. To compress a drive other than the current drive, choose Choose Drive. Choose **B**egin Compress to compress the current drive.

9. A warning appears instructing you to remove memory-resident programs and to back up your disk before running Compress.

- If you need to remove memory-resident programs or back up your disk, choose Cancel to return to the Compress screen, then press F3 to return to DOS.
- To proceed with the compression, choose **C**ompress again. Then choose **O**K to confirm.

10. Compression begins. The drive map changes as sectors are read, then written to optimum locations on the disk. When the compression is finished, you are given the following options:

    - Choose **M**irror to save Mirror information. This option updates the Mirror file to reflect the new arrangements of directories and files. Always use this option.
    - Choose Exit to return to the DOS prompt.
    - Choose C**o**ntinue to return to the Compress screen.

11. Reboot your computer.

Warning Do not turn off your computer during compression operations. Data can be lost if you do. Press Escape to exit Compress safely.

Always reboot your computer after a compression operation. Your files and directories have been rearranged. Your applications may look for them in their previous locations. This can cause loss of data and destroy hard-disk formatting information.

To Choose an Ordering Method

1. Load Compress. Pull down the **O**ptions menu.
2. Choose **O**rdering Methods.
3. Choose one of the following options:

   Standard places directories at the beginning of the disk, then places your files in any order. Unless you specify otherwise, directories are placed in the order they appear in the PATH statement of your AUTOEXEC.BAT file.

   File Placement places directories first, then places files as specified with the Files To Place First command.

Directories First places directories at the beginning of the disk in the order specified (if any) with the Directory Order command, followed by files arranged by directory (see "To Specify the Order of Directories"). This option provides maximum optimization because data and program files are located close to one another.

Directories With Files positions each directory or subdirectory in front of its files. Use this method if you normally create and delete entire subdirectories rather than individual files.

To Specify the Order of Directories

1. Load Compress and pull down the **O**ptions menu.
2. Choose Directory Order. The Directory Ordering dialog box appears. The Directory Tree box on the left displays the current directory structure. The Path box on the right displays the current order of directories on your disk.
   - To add directories from the directory tree to the path list, select the directory, then choose **A**dd. Once directories are in the path list, they can be moved or deleted.
   - To move a directory in the path list, select the directory you want to move, then choose **M**ove. Use arrow keys or the mouse to move the directory to where you want it.
   - To delete a directory from the path list, select the directory you want to delete, then choose **D**elete. This does not delete the directory from your disk; it removes the directory from the specified order. Compress places directories deleted from the path list according to standard specifications.
3. Choose **O**K.

Use the Directory Order command to optimize disk access for the directories you use most often. Move the directories you use most often to the top of the directory tree, then run Compress using the Directories First or Directories With Files option. Frequently accessed directories are placed at the beginning of the disk for easier access.

To Specify Files to Place First

1. Load Compress and pull down the **Options** menu.
2. Choose **Files To Place First**. A dialog box appears.
3. Enter file specifications. Use the * wildcard to represent groups of characters. Use ? to represent individual characters.
4. Choose **OK**.

Use the Files To Place First command in conjunction with the File Placement option.

Tip Move frequently accessed files to the beginning of the disk to increase overall disk performance.

To Specify the Order of Files within Directories

1. Load Compress and pull down the **Options** menu.
2. Choose **File Sort Options**. The Choose Sort Method dialog box appears. Choose one sort key: **Date/Time**, **File Name**, **Extension**, or **Size**.
3. Choose a sort order: **No Sorting**, **Ascending**, or **Descending**.
4. Choose **OK**.

When you choose any sort key other than File Name, file names are used as a secondary sort key. For example, if you choose Extension as a sort key, all files are sorted by extension, then all files with common extensions are sorted by name.

To Analyze Your Disk for Optimization

1. Load Compress and pull down the **Analysis** menu.
2. To display a summary of file allocations, choose **Disk Statistics**. The Disk Statistics message box appears, giving you information about allocated and unallocated clusters, bad clusters, file chains, the percentage of file fragmentation,

free space areas, cross-linked files, unattached files, and bad clusters within files. In addition, a compression method is recommended, if needed.

3. To display fragmentation information about individual files, choose **F**ile Fragmentation Analysis. Move to the desired directory in the directory tree, then select a file from the file list. Next to each file name is the total number of clusters the file occupies, the number of contiguous areas it occupies, and its percentage of fragmentation.

4. To display a list of the clusters and files within individual blocks on the disk map, choose **S**how Files In Each Map Block. The cursor moves to the disk map. Position it on the block you want to analyze. Press Enter or click with the mouse to display its contents.

• OPTIONS Several pull-down menu commands are available as function-key commands from the message bar at the bottom of the screen. To invoke a command quickly, press the function key or click on the command name.

F4 (Begin)	Executes the Begin Compress option from the Compress menu
F5 (Analyze)	Executes the Disk Statistics option from the Analysis menu
F6 (Technique)	Executes the Compression Technique option from the Options menu
F7 (Methods)	Executes the Ordering Methods option from the Options menu
F8 (DirOrdr)	Executes the Directory Order option from the Options menu
F9 (Sort)	Executes the File Sort Options option from the Options menu

To Load Compress from DOS or a Batch File

At the DOS prompt or in a batch file, such as your AUTOEXEC.BAT file, enter the Compress command in the following format:

COMPRESS *drive /options*

where *drive* is the letter of the drive to be compressed (if no drive letter is entered, the current drive is compressed) and */options* is one or more of the command-line options described below. You must specify a Compress option in your AUTOEXEC.BAT file so that the program runs without further input.

• **OPTIONS** Enter one or more of the following slash (/) commands to specify the type of compression you want:

/CC Performs a full compression and wipes all unused sectors

/CD Moves directories to the beginning of the disk but does not unfragment files

/CF Performs a full compression

/CS Optimizes free space but does not unfragment files

/CU Unfragments files but does not consolidate free space

/NM Disables Mirror after Compress is finished

/OD Places each directory just before the files it contains

/OF Places directories, then files specified with the Files To Place First command, then all other files

/OO Places all directories at the beginning of the disk, then files grouped according to directory

/OS Places directories at the beginning of the disk, then their files in order of creation/modification

/SA Sorts files in ascending order; can be used with another sort option

/SD Sorts files in descending order; can be used with another sort option

/SE Sorts files by extension

/SF	Sorts files by name
/SS	Sorts files by size
/ST	Sorts files by date/time attribute

• **NOTE** You can schedule Compress to run automatically at specified times by using the Appointment Scheduler. To do this, enter a command line (as described in the section above) in the Description text box of the Make Appointment dialog box.

CONVERT

The Convert utility translates setup files from other backup programs (such as FastBack and Norton Backup) to a format readable by CP Backup, PC Tools' backup program.

To Convert Setup Files to CP Backup Format

At the DOS prompt, enter the Convert command in the following format:

CONVERT *drive /options*

where *drive* is the disk drive you want to search for setup files and */options* is one or more of the options described below.

• **OPTIONS** Enter one or more of the following options (preceded by the backslash) to configure your conversion operation.

/CPBACKUP	Searches for setup files created by CP Backup
/DEST=*directory*	Specifies the directory to which you want to write your converted setup files
/FASTBACK	Searches for setup files created by FastBack

/NORTON	Searches for setup files created by Norton Backup
/PROMPT	Displays a prompt asking you to confirm each conversion
/QUIET	Performs conversions without writing anything to your screen

CP BACKUP

The CP Backup utility creates backup copies of all or part of your disks. CP Backup allows you to

- Create full backups of entire disks
- Create backups of selected directories, subdirectories, and files
- Schedule backups for specified intervals
- Compress data as it is being backed up to save space
- Create incremental backups of only files changed since the last backup
- Verify the readability of your backups
- Recover backed up disks, directories, and files

Warning Creating backups is a crucial computing operation. Disk crashes, file incompatibilities, and other unpredictable circumstances can cause you to lose data requiring weeks or months to recover—or that may be impossible to recover. As a rule of thumb, make full backups either weekly or monthly, then smaller backups on a daily basis. To decide how often to create backups, ask yourself, "How much data can I afford to lose?" Always create full backups when moving your computer or when sending it in for service (especially hard-drive service).

Also, consider keeping a set of backup disks at a remote location (such as in a safe-deposit box). Then, if a fire destroys both your computer and your backup disks, you can still recover most of your data on a replacement machine.

To Load CP Backup

1. At the DOS prompt, enter the command

   CPBACKUP

   The program is loaded. If Express mode is enabled, the Express interface appears.
2. Choose **B**ackup to start a backup operation or to configure CP Backup on your machine. The Backup main menu window appears.

When Express mode is enabled (the default), an additional Backup window is displayed. This window presents the Backup commands used most frequently in a quick, convenient format.

To Specify Configuration Options

1. From the main Backup window, pull down the **C**onfigure menu.
2. To specify drive and media for backup and restoration operations, choose Define **E**quipment. A dialog box appears, asking whether there is a tape drive connected to your system. Choose **Y**es or **N**o. If you choose No, go to step 3. If you choose Yes, another dialog box appears, giving you two options:
   - Choose **S**earch if your tape drive is connected to your floppy-disk controller. The program searches your system for tape drives it recognizes and supports.
   - Choose **C**onfigure if your tape drive is connected to a secondary controller card. A new dialog box appears. Using hexadecimal values, enter the port address, interrupt request level (IRQ), and the number of the Direct Memory Access (DMA) channel for your tape controller card.

3. The Define Equipment window appears, listing all drives on your system. Choose drive and capacity, if needed, to reflect your system's configuration. Then choose **O**K.

4. The Choose Drive & Media dialog box appears, listing your system drives and the capacities specified in step 3. Choose the drives to which you want to write your backups. If you choose Fixed Drive And Path, you are prompted to enter a DOS drive and path. Then choose **O**K.

5. To specify backup speed, pull down the **C**onfigure menu and choose **B**ackup Speed. Then choose one of the following options:

   High Speed uses the DMA controller to read and write data simultaneously from your hard disk to a floppy or tape drive. This is the fastest option but works only when backing up to drives A and B or supported tape drives.

   Medium Speed uses the DMA controller but does not read and write simultaneously. This option can be used with floppy and tape drives.

   Low Speed (DOS Compatible) uses the microprocessor instead of the DMA controller. This is the slowest option; it can be used with any type of DOS device.

6. Choose **O**K to accept your selections, or choose **C**ancel to return to the Configure menu. Choose **T**est to perform a confidence test of medium- and high-speed backups. Follow prompts and insert disks as required. When the test is completed, a message window summarizes the results and CP Backup is automatically configured to the highest recommended speed setting.

7. To specify user level, pull down the **C**onfigure menu and choose **U**ser Level. Then choose one of the following options:

   Beginner uses default settings only; you cannot change backup methods, select files, or choose options. This is the safest, easiest backup level.

   Intermediate allows you to change backup methods and select files, and gives you a limited choice of options.

   Advanced allows you to change all options.

Express Mode disables the Express interface, which is the dialog box that appears each time you load CP Backup.

• NOTES The commands available from the Options menu change with each user level.

The first time you run CP Backup, a confidence test is run on your hard and floppy drives to determine the optimum backup speed for your system.

Warning Backups done at high or medium speeds cannot be restored at low speed. Always use low-speed backups if you are restoring your data on another computer that may not be capable of restoring at the higher speed settings.

Shortcut To display the Choose Drive & Media and Define Equipment dialog boxes quickly, press the F7 and F8 keys, respectively.

• OPTIONS The options discussed here reflect all commands available from the Options menu that have not been previously discussed in this section. Some of these are available from the main Backup window. The availability of these commands varies according to user level. (See "To Specify a Backup Method" and "To Specify Configuration Options" above.)

Reporting Presents three options for generating a summary report of backup activities:

None turns off the reporting option (the default).

Report To Printer sends a report to your printer.

Report To File creates a disk file of the report.

Compress Presents three options for compressing data as it is backed up, thus reducing the amount of media space (tape or disks) required:

None turns off the compression option.

Minimize Time compresses data as much as possible without slowing down the backup operation (the default).

Minimize Space-Moderate performs a moderate compression of data; backup is slowed but required media space is reduced.

Minimize Space-Maximum reduces media space and slows the overall operation, more than any other option.

Verify Presents three options for checking that the data written to your backup media can be read:

None turns off the Verify option.

When Formatting checks media after formatting (the default).

Always checks data each time data is backed up.

Media Format Presents four options for formatting backup media in CPS (Central Point Software proprietary format) or standard formats:

CPS Floppy Format formats disks by using proprietary Central Point formatting. Disks hold more data than in standard format, so the backup requires fewer disks. But these disks cannot be read by DOS.

DOS Standard Format uses standard DOS formatting (the default for disk backups). This option requires more disks than CPS formatting, but disks can be read by DOS.

CPS Tape Format formats tapes by using proprietary Central Point formatting (the default for tape backups). Allows you to pause and resume backups, and to use incremental backups with tapes.

QIC Compatible Format formats tapes by using the standard QIC format.

Format Always Formats backup media each time you create a backup (the default is Off).

Error Correction Stores error correction information on the backup media, significantly increasing the chances of recovering data if media is damaged. This option increases the time required for backups (the default is On).

Virus Detection Scans all selected directories and files for viruses (the default is Off). If infected files are found, you are given three options:

Continue backs up all selected, including infected, files.

Rename gives infected files a .V*nn* extension, where *nn* is a sequential number between 00 and 99, and excludes them from backup.

Cancel stops the backup operation.

Save History Writes the backup history file to your hard disk. A history file containing a list of backed-up files, time of backup, and backup type is written to your backup media for each operation. Writing the file to your hard disk speeds up restoration and comparison operations. This option is not available for low-speed backups (the default is On).

Overwrite Warning Displays messages alerting you that your backup disk has been used for a previous backup or that existing files on your hard disk may be overwritten during a restoration (the default is On).

Time Display Turns on (and off) a display of time elapsed during backups (the default is On).

Display Options, Sort Options Presents the following options for sorting the tree list (the default is Unsorted):

Unsorted lists files in their physical order on the disk.

By Name lists files sorted in alphabetical order by name.

By Extension lists files sorted by file extension.

By Date lists files in ascending date order (newest to oldest).

By Size lists files in ascending order by size (largest to smallest)

Sort Descending reverses the order of the sorts above.

Display Options, Long Format Changes the file list to display size, date/time of creation, and attributes of each file (The default is Off).

To Select Directories and Files for Backup

1. Display the directory tree. There are three ways to do this:
   - Double-click on the drive in the Backup From window.
   - Pull down the Action menu and choose Choose Directories.

- Disable the Express Mode option. To do this, choose User Level from the Configure menu. Then choose Express Mode.

2. Use the arrow keys or the mouse to select directories and files for backup.

• OPTIONS You can also select files automatically by using the following commands, available from the Options menu in intermediate and advanced user levels. When any of these options is enabled, a check mark appears next to it on the menu. Make automatic selections before you make manual selections.

Subdirectory inclusion includes all subdirectories within selected directories (the default is On).

Include/Exclude files displays a text window you can use to select or unselect files according to file specifications. You are allowed up to 16 lines of specifications, and each line is processed in order from top to bottom. Use the * wildcard to represent groups of characters and the ? wildcard to represent individual characters. Use the minus sign (–) to exclude specifications. The default is *.*. See the example below.

Attribute exclusions displays a dialog box you can use to exclude files with hidden, system, and read-only file attributes (the default for all three attributes is Off).

Date range selection displays another dialog box you can use to specify a range of dates and back up only files created within this range.

• EXAMPLE Suppose you want to create a backup of all the files in your \WP51 directory with .DOC extensions, all the files in your \DBASE directory with .DBF extensions, and all the files in your \123 directory with .WK1 extensions. Also, suppose you have created subdirectories for each directory according to the projects you work on.

To do this, first enable the Subdirectory Inclusion option (a check mark is displayed next to the option). Choose the Include/Exclude Files command, and enter the following lines in the window:

\WP51*.DOC

\DBASE*.DBF

\123*.WK1

Because you have turned on Subdirectory Inclusion, there is no need to enter the specifications for each subdirectory. All files with the specified extensions are included in the backup, regardless of the subdirectory in which they reside.

To Specify a Backup Method

1. Choose a backup method option—there are two ways:
   - Choose **M**ethod from the main Backup window (if you have the Express interface on). A pull-down menu appears, listing the available options.
   - Pull down the **O**ptions menu and choose **B**ackup Method. The Backup Method dialog box appears, listing the available options.

   Here are the backup method options:

   Full backs up all selected files in all selected directories, regardless of whether they have been changed since the last backup. This option also clears the archive attribute of all backed-up files. Use this option at regular intervals, when moving your computer, or when servicing a hard drive.

   Incremental reads the archive attribute of files and backs up only files that, according to this attribute, have been changed or are newly created since the last full backup. An incremental backup is appended to the full backup; the new data is written to the end of the full backup disks. Archive attributes of all backed-up files are reset. Use this option at frequent intervals between full backups.

   Differential backs up only files that have been changed since the last backup. Differential backups always start on a new disk and overwrite data that may be on any disk. The archive attribute of backed-up files does not change.

Full Copy backs up all selected files in all selected directories but does not change their archive attribute. Use this option to make multiple copies of full backups.

Separate Incremental backs up files the same as an incremental backup but does not append the backup to the full backup disks. Use this option to make multiple copies of incremental backups.

Virus Scan Only scans your hard drive for the presence of viruses. Use this option at regular intervals and always before performing full backups.

2. If you have chosen backup methods from the Options menu, choose OK to continue, or choose Cancel to return to the Options menu.

To Start a Backup

1. Choose Start Backup.
2. If you are backing up to disks, go to step 4. If you are backing up to tape, insert a tape in the drive.
3. A dialog box appears listing all backups that have been written to the tape. Choose OK to continue, Erase to erase the tape, New Tape to indicate a previously unused tape, or Cancel to return to the main menu.
4. The Name Backup Set dialog box appears. Enter a descriptive name for the backup operation (30 characters maximum). This description appears in the Choose Directory dialog box and the History file.
5. Enter a password, if desired.
6. Choose OK to begin backing up your data. If you are using disks, insert disks as prompted.

Keep in mind that the easiest, safest way to perform backups is to set the user level mode to Beginner, then simply use the default configuration. You can press Escape anytime you want to pause or cancel a backup operation.

To Save a Setup File

1. Pull down the File menu and choose Save Setup to overwrite the current setup file, or choose Save Setup As to create a new setup file. The Save Current Settings dialog box appears.
2. Enter a name for the current configuration.
3. Check the Save File Selections box to save directory and file selections made from the tree list.
4. Choose OK to save the setup file, or choose Cancel to return to the Backup window.

To Load a Setup File

1. Pull down the File menu and choose Load Setup. The Load Setup File dialog box appears, listing all available setup files.
2. Use the mouse or arrow keys to move the highlight to the setup file you want to load. Press Enter.
3. Choose OK to load the selected setup file, or choose Cancel to return to the Backup window. Choose Delete to remove the selected file from the list.

To Schedule Automatic Backups

You can use the Scheduler, without leaving CP Backup, to automate your backups. This option is especially convenient if you are backing up to tapes, because backups can be run completely unattended. A good strategy is to alternate tapes (or sets of disks) for each backup so that you never write over your most recent backup copy. For example, use tape A for even-numbered weeks and tape B for odd-numbered weeks.

1. Configure a setup file for the backup operation you want to schedule. Suggestion: Use WEEKLY for your full backups and DAILY for your incremental backups, depending on how often you run them.
2. From the Backup window, choose Scheduler.

3. Enter the name of the existing setup file in the appropriate box.
4. Select the day or days the backup is to be run.
5. Enter a time for the backup to be run in the appropriate box.
6. Choose **OK**.
7. Choose **Add** to schedule another backup. Choose **Modify** to edit an existing entry. Choose **Save** to save your changes and return to the main menu. Choose **Cancel** to return to the main menu without saving your changes.

To Load CP Backup from DOS or a Batch File

The easiest way to run CP Backup from DOS or in a batch file, such as your AUTOEXEC.BAT file, is to create a setup file first. Then, using the format that follows, enter the CP Backup command line at the DOS prompt or add it to your batch file:

BACKUP *(setup filename)*

The backup operation runs automatically using the configuration options specified in your setup file (see "To Save a Setup File" and "To Load a Setup File").

As an alternative, you can enter command-line options to configure your backup operation. See your Central Point manuals for more information.

To Restore Backed Up Data

You can use CP Backup to restore your entire hard disk or selected directories and files. In addition, you can restore files backed up from one machine on a different machine. Restoration operations must be configured using the same speed as the original backup. Indeed, the way you restore files depends a great deal on how you backed them up. If you created a setup file when you made your backup, use the same setup file when restoring files. Refer to the procedures above for more information.

Warning When restoring files, you can overwrite existing files of the same name—even if the existing files are newer than the restored files. By doing this, you lose data created since the backup. To prevent unwanted data loss, enable the Overwrite Warning command from the Options menu before restoring files.

To Fully Restore a Disk

1. At the DOS prompt, enter the command

   CPBACKUP

   The program is loaded, and the Central Point Backup opening window appears.

2. Choose **R**estore to start a restoration or to configure CP Backup on your machine. The Restore window appears.

3. Choose **R**estore From. Select the drive from which files are to be restored.

4. Choose Restore **T**o. Select the drive to which files are to be restored.

5. Choose Retrieve History. Insert the last disk or the tape of the backup set as prompted.

6. Choose Start Restore. Insert disks or tapes as prompted. Restoration begins. A summary of the operation's progress is displayed.

Use this procedure in the unfortunate event you lose your entire drive. You must first install DOS and the CP Backup program. In addition, if you want to use the mouse for the restoration, you must install your mouse driver. See the appropriate installation manuals for more information.

To Restore from Full and Partial Backups

You may need to restore your hard disk using a full backup and subsequent partial (differential or incremental) backups. Depending on the backup method you use, there are several ways to restore your disk:

- If you make incremental backups, you need only do a single restoration because each incremental backup is appended to the full backup set.

- If you make separate incremental backups, you can first restore your full backup set, then each separate incremental backup.
- If you make differential backups, you can restore the last differential backup first, then the full backup.

Follow these steps:

1. Follow steps 1 to 6 in "To Fully Restore a Disk," if required.
2. Choose Retrieve History. Insert the last disk or the requested tape of the separate incremental backup set when prompted. The history file is read and stored.
3. Choose Start **R**estore. Insert the separate incremental disks or tapes as prompted.
4. Repeat steps 2 and 3 until all separate incremental back-ups have been restored.

When Overwrite Warning is turned on, a dialog box is displayed each time the restoration encounters a file of the same name. Choose Overwrite With **N**ewer File Only and **R**epeat For All Later Files to restore only the latest versions of files.

To Restore Only Selected Files

You can use the Search History command to restore selected files if a directory or file is accidentally wiped out. To do this, history files must be saved on your hard disk. (Save files on your hard disk by turning on the Save History command from the Options menu.)

1. From the Restore window, choose Search History. The Search History dialog box appears.
2. In the upper field, enter file specifications for the files you want to restore. Use the DOS wildcards * and ?, and separate each specification with a space or a comma. For example, to search for files with .DOC and .WK1 extensions, enter ***.DOC, *.WK1**.
3. Enter a range of file creation/modification dates from which you want to search files. This option can be skipped.

4. Select one or more history files you want to search. Choose Select **All** to search all history files. Then choose **Search** to continue. The located files are displayed.

5. Unselect files as needed. Then choose **Load** to restore these files.

CP BACKUP FOR WINDOWS

CP Backup for Windows creates and restore backups from the Windows environment. While the look of Backup for Windows differs from the DOS version, the menus, dialog boxes, and command sequences are virtually identical to those of the DOS version. See CP Backup for step-by-step procedures for running Backup for Windows.

• NOTES The list that follows describes the main differences between CP Backup and CP Backup For Windows:

- The Printer Setup command allows you to configure your printer from within Undelete. A handy feature of this command allows you to specify how extended characters are printed.
- The Backup From command is not available from the Action menu. Select the backup drive from the Backup From box of the main window.
- The Time Display command is not available from the Options menu.
- The Express Mode option is not available.

See Also *CP Backup*

CPBDIR

CPBDIR is a standalone utility program that displays helpful information about backup disks formatted with the Central Point proprietary formatting method. This information includes the number of disks, the correct order of disks, and configuration settings.

To Display Information about CPS-Formatted Disks

At the DOS prompt, enter the command

CPBDIR *drive /x*

where *drive* is the drive in which the backup disk is inserted, and */x* enables an extended display of information about the backup disks.

CPSCHED

The Central Point Scheduler utility must be memory-resident before you can automate Backup and Commute sessions. You can install the Scheduler from the DOS prompt, from your AUTOEXEC.BAT or other batch file, or by choosing Load Scheduler during installation.

To Load CPSCHED

At the DOS prompt, enter the command

CPSCHED

• **NOTE** Use the Kill utility to remove the Scheduler from memory.

CP SCHEDULER FOR WINDOWS

The CP Scheduler for Windows program allows you to run other programs automatically. You can schedule Backup and Commute sessions and regular DiskFix analyses to maintain optimum hard-drive performance.

To Start Scheduler for Windows

1. Click on the Scheduler icon from the Windows desktop.
2. Choose **B**ackup, Commute, or **D**iskFix.

To Schedule Backup and Commute Sessions

1. From the Schedule window, choose **A**dd to create a new entry, **M**odify to edit an entry, or **D**elete to remove an entry.
2. If you choose Add, an Add New Item dialog box appears. Choose **S**cript File or **Se**tup File to specify a setup file for a Backup session or a script file for a Commute session.
3. Specify a time for the session. Choose **T**ime and enter a time. Or use the left scroll arrows to set the hour and right scroll arrows to set minutes.
4. Specify the day or days the program is to run. Choose **D**ay Of The Week and select one or more days. Choose **OK**.
5. Choose E**n**able Backup Events or E**n**able Commute Events. These options allow scheduled events to occur while Windows is running. If this option is off, scheduled events are ignored.
6. Choose **OK**.

To Schedule DiskFix

1. From the main Scheduler window, choose DiskFix. The DiskFix Schedule dialog box appears.
2. Press Alt-R and specify an interval setting in the Run Disk-Fix Every *nn* Minutes field.
3. Move the cursor to the Starting At field and enter a time. Use the left arrows to set hour and the right arrows to set minutes.
4. Move to the Ending At field and enter a time. Use the left arrows to set hour and the right arrows to set minutes.
5. Choose Drives to select drives for analysis by DiskFix.
6. Choose Enable DiskFix Events to allow scheduled disk fixes while Windows is running.
7. Choose OK.

• **NOTES** The Scheduler must be active for scheduled sessions to be run. If you exit the program, you deactivate the Scheduler. For this reason, when you choose Exit from the File menu, a dialog box appears and gives you these options:

OK quits the program and deactivates all scheduled events.

Cancel returns you to the Scheduler window.

Minimize closes the window without exiting the program. Use this option to keep all schedules active. The Scheduler icon remains on the desktop.

The PC Tools installation program configures Windows so that the Scheduler is activated each time the program is run.

DATA MONITOR

Data Monitor is a memory-resident program that provides powerful options for guarding against data loss, preventing unauthorized data access, and indicating disk read/write operations:

Delete Protection guards against data loss.

Screen Blanker prevents screen burn-in and protects the confidentiality of on-screen data.

Directory Lock prevents access to selected directories.

Write Protection protects crucial files from malicious or accidental deletions, overwrites, or damage.

Disk Light installs an on-screen indicator that is displayed when any drive is accessed.

To Load Data Monitor

At the DOS prompt, enter the command

DATAMON

The program is loaded, and the Data Monitor main window appears.

To Install Delete Protection

1. From the Data Monitor main menu, choose Delete Protection.
2. Choose one of two options:

   Delete Sentry creates a hidden directory named \SENTRY and moves all deleted files to it. With this option turned on, Undelete has an excellent chance of recovering files because their directory entry and the data contained within them are changed but not removed.

   Delete Tracker keeps a record of the cluster locations of deleted files. With this information, Undelete has a good chance of recovering files deleted accidentally.

3. Choose **OK** to continue. If you are using Delete Tracker, go to step 6.
4. If you chose Delete Sentry in step 2, a dialog box appears prompting you to specify these Sentry options:

   All Files protects all files.

   Only Specified Files protects only files specified in the Include and Exclude list boxes. To include or exclude files, use the DOS wildcards * and ? to enter specifications for each box.

   Do Not Save Archived Files protects only files for which the archive attribute has been cleared, indicating that they have been changed since the last backup.

   Purge Files After *n* Days removes files from the \SENTRY directory after the *n*th day.

   Limit Disk Space For Deleted Files To *nn*% specifies the amount of disk space reserved for the hidden directory (20% is the default). When files stored in the \SENTRY directory exceed *nn*%, they are purged automatically in the order in which they are saved (oldest to most recent).
5. Choose **Drives** to specify which drives are protected by Delete Sentry.
6. Use the arrow keys or mouse to select drives, then choose **OK**. If you chose Delete Tracker, the program returns to the main menu.
7. Choose **OK** to save your changes, or choose **Cancel** to return to the Data Monitor menu without saving.

Data Monitor provides two methods for protecting your files against unwanted deletion, Delete Sentry and Delete Tracker. Of the two, Delete Sentry provides almost foolproof recoverability but takes up disk space. Delete Tracker is less reliable, but provides excellent recoverability as long as deleted files are not overwritten.

To Install the Screen Blanker

1. From the Data Monitor main menu, choose **Screen Blanker**.

2. Choose Load Screen Blanker. By choosing this option, the Screen Blanker is loaded when you exit Data Monitor.
3. In the appropriate box, specify the number of minutes before the screen is blanked.
4. To create a password that must be entered before the screen is restored, choose **P**assword. Enter the password in the appropriate box, then choose **O**K.
5. To change the hotkey used to clear the screen immediately, choose **H**otkey. Hold down the Ctrl or Alt key, and press the key you want to complete the combination. Ctrl-Z is the default. Press Enter to save the new hotkey setting. Press Escape to disable the hotkey.
6. Choose **O**K to save the new Screen Blanker configuration, or choose **C**ancel to return to the Data Monitor menu without saving changes.

Use the Screen Blanker to prevent images from being "burned in" on your monitor. If the same image is displayed for a long enough time, a faint ghost image of it may be permanently displayed. When your system is idle for a specified period, Screen Blanker clears your screen until you restore it by pressing any key.

To Install Directory Locks

1. From the Data Monitor main menu, choose D**i**rectory Lock.
2. Choose Load Directory Lock. (By choosing this option, Directory Lock is loaded when you exit Data Monitor.)
3. Enter the name of the directory or directories you want password-protected in the **D**irectory Name To Protect text box. Do not enter backslashes (\).
4. Move to **T**imeout Period. Enter the number of minutes the computer can be idle before the password is requested again. Set this value to 0 or leave it blank if you want to be requested to enter the password only once a session.
5. Move to **W**ait For Password. Enter the number of seconds the program waits for you to enter the password before quitting.

6. Choose **P**assword. Enter the new password. Then choose **OK**.
7. Choose **N**etwork to specify a network drive for protection.
8. Choose **OK** to save your changes, or choose **C**ancel to return to the Data Monitor main menu without saving your changes.

If you turn on Directory Lock for a specified directory, all files are automatically encrypted and decrypted as they are written to and read from that directory—provided the appropriate password is used.

To Install Write Protection

1. From the Data Monitor main window, choose **W**rite Protection. The Write Protection dialog box appears.
2. Choose **L**oad Write Protection. (By choosing this option, Write Protection is loaded when you exit Data Monitor.)
3. Choose from the following options:

   Entire Disk protects your entire disk, including system areas, the file allocation tables, directories, and unused free space, unless you confirm each write operation yourself.

   System Areas protects the boot records, the hard-disk partition table, and file allocation tables.

   File Types Listed Below protects files as specified in the Include and Exclude boxes.

   Protect Removable Drives Also protects peripheral drives also.
4. If you turned on the File Types Listed Below option, specify files to be included and excluded in the appropriate boxes. Use DOS wildcards (* and ?) to specify file groups.
5. Choose **OK** to save your changes, or choose **C**ancel to return to the Data Monitor window without saving.

Write Protection prevents important files from being overwritten, deleted, or damaged.

To Install the Disk Light

1. From the Data Monitor window, choose Disk **L**ight.

2. Choose **Load Disk Light**. (By choosing this option, the disk light is loaded when you exit Data Monitor.)

3. Choose **OK** to save your changes, or choose **Cancel** to return to the Data Monitor window without saving.

Use the Disk Light option to install a disk-access light in the upper-right corner of your screen. This option is useful if you use a tower configuration, work on a network, or the disk-access light on your CPU is difficult to see.

Tip To display a report listing all the Data Monitor options you have chosen, choose **Summary** from the main menu.

To Load Data Monitor from DOS or a Batch File

Enter a command line in the following format either at the DOS prompt or within a batch file, such as AUTOEXEC.BAT:

DATAMON */option+* **or** */option–*

where */option+* turns on and */option–* turns off the specified options as follows:

DATALOCK enables Directory Lock.

LIGHT enables Disk Light.

TRACKER enables Delete Protection and Delete Tracker method.

SENTRY enables Delete Protection and Delete Sentry method.

WRITE enables Write Protection.

SCREEN enables the Screen Blanker.

- **OPTIONS** You can also add the following command-line options:

/UNLOAD Unloads Data Monitor from memory if it was the last TSR loaded; otherwise, it disables it

/STATUS Displays the summary report of all Data Monitor options

/?	Displays a help screen listing Data Monitor command-line options

DESKCONNECT

The DeskConnect utility allows you to connect two computers, usually your desktop machine and a remote machine, such as a laptop. You can then transfer files between the computers just as you would from one drive to another on a single system. For detailed procedures on loading and running DeskConnect, see the DeskConnect command in Part 1.

See Also *DeskConnect* (Part 1)

DIRECTORY MAINTENANCE

The Directory Maintenance utility creates, edits, deletes, and moves directories and subdirectories throughout the directory tree structure. (Many Directory Maintenance commands are available from PC Shell.)

To Open Directory Maintenance

At the DOS prompt, enter the command

DM

The main Directory Maintenance window appears. This window consists of a tree structure representation of the current drive and its directories.

• **OPTIONS** Once the Directory Maintenance window is opened, the following function-key commands are available from the message bar at the bottom of the screen:

F1 (Help)	Displays help screens
F2 (Reread)	Rereads the directory tree
F3 (Exit)	Quits Directory Maintenance and returns to PC Shell
F4 (Make)	Makes new directory
F5 (Rename)	Changes name of selected directory
F6 (Delete)	Deletes selected directory
F7 (Prune)	Takes a directory and all its subdirectories and grafts them to another branch
F8 (Files)	Toggles list of files in current directory
F9 (Copy)	Copies directory branch
F10 (Menu)	Activates pull-down menus

To Rename a Volume (Drive)

1. Pull down the Volume menu.
2. Choose Rename Volume.
3. Enter the new volume name, then choose OK.

To Change Drives

1. Pull down the Volume menu.
2. Choose Change Drive.
3. Click on or press the letter of the drive you want to select.
4. Choose OK.

Shortcut To change drives quickly, click the drive you want to activate on the drive line (in the upper-left corner of the window, just below the menu bar), or simply press Ctrl and the drive letter.

To Change Directories

1. Begin typing the name of the directory to which you want to go. The highlight moves, with each keystroke, to the directory corresponding to the letters you type. Thus, you may only have to enter a few letters to move to your desired directory.
2. Press Enter when the highlight is on your desired directory to exit Directory Maintenance. You are returned to PC Shell, and the directory you selected is activated.

Shortcut To change directories quickly, click once on the selected directory.

To Reread the Directory Tree

1. From the Directory Maintenance window, pull down the Volume menu.
2. Choose Reread Tree.

Use the Reread Tree command to update your directory tree if you use DOS to create or change the directory structure.

To View Files in a Selected Directory

1. Select the directory for which you want to view a file list.
2. Pull down the Directory menu.
3. Choose Show Files. A scrollable window appears listing all files in the selected directory.
4. To close the file list, press Escape or click anywhere outside the window.

To Create a New Directory

1. Select the directory to which you want to add a subdirectory.
2. Pull down the **D**irectory menu.
3. Choose **M**ake Directory. The Make Directory dialog box appears.
4. Enter a new name for the subdirectory.
5. Choose **OK** to save your changes, or choose **Cancel** to return to the main menu without saving.

Shortcut Once you have selected a directory, you can quickly display the Make Directory dialog box by pressing F4 or clicking the Make command on the message bar.

• **NOTES** Directory names can be up to eight characters and can have a three-character extension separated by a period. The name cannot contain spaces, commas, periods, or backslashes. Valid characters include the letters A though Z, the numbers 0 through 9, and a number of special characters (for a complete list, see "Directory Maintenance" in Part 1).

Two subdirectories in the same directory cannot have the same name. Subdirectories in different directories can have the same name.

To Rename a Directory

1. Select the directory you want to rename (the root directory cannot be renamed).
2. Pull down the **D**irectory menu.
3. Choose **R**ename Directory. The Rename Directory dialog box appears.
4. Enter a new name for the directory.
5. Choose **OK** to save your changes, or choose **Cancel** to return to the main menu without saving.

Shortcut Once you have selected a directory, you can quickly display the Rename Directory dialog box by pressing F5 or clicking the Rename command on the message bar.

To Delete a Directory

1. Select the directory you want to delete. (You cannot delete the root directory of a system disk.)
2. Pull down the **Directory** menu.
3. Choose **Delete Directory**.
4. If the directory you have selected contains files, a warning message appears. Choose **OK** to delete the directory and all its files, or choose **Cancel** to return to the main menu without deleting the directory.

Shortcut Once you have selected a directory, you can quickly invoke the Delete command by pressing F6 or clicking the Delete command on the message bar.

To Move a Directory Using Prune And Graft

1. From the tree list, select the directory you want to move.
2. Pull down the **Directory** menu.
3. Choose Prune And **Graft**.
4. If you want to move the directory to another drive, select that drive now. The directory tree for the new drive appears.
5. Move the directory to the desired location on the tree list, either by using the arrow keys or by clicking and dragging using the mouse.
6. When the directory is in the desired location, press F7 or double-click with the mouse.
7. Choose **OK** to confirm the new location for the directory.

To Change the Attributes of a Directory

1. Pull down the Directory menu.
2. Choose Modify Attributes.
3. From the tree list, select the directory you want to modify. The Modify Attributes dialog box appears.
4. Choose Hidden or System. If you choose Hidden, the directory is concealed from the DIR command in DOS and from PC Shell in beginner mode. The directory is visible in Directory Maintenance. If you choose System, the directory is concealed from the DIR command in DOS and from PC Shell in beginner mode. The directory is visible in Directory Maintenance. Under normal circumstances, this attribute is not used.

• **NOTES** The root directory has no attributes.

Network directory attributes cannot be changed.

Changing the attributes of system directories can prevent your hard drive from booting. In addition, many programs create temporary files or write to data files as they are run. Changing attributes of program directories may affect their ability to run properly. In addition, changing a directory's attributes affects the way it is displayed and may prevent you from writing to that directory.

To Copy a Directory

1. From the tree list, select the directory you want to copy.
2. Pull down the Directory menu.
3. Choose Copy Tree or press F9. A copy of the selected directory appears on the tree.
4. Use the arrow keys or mouse to position the directory where you want to copy it.
5. Press F9.
6. Choose OK to confirm copying.

To Load Directory Maintenance from DOS or a Batch File

Enter a command line in the following format at the DOS prompt or within your batch file, such as AUTOEXEC.BAT:

DM *drive directory /options*

• **OPTIONS** Use the following options when entering a Directory Maintenance command line:

drive	Specifies the drive for which the tree list is displayed. All other commands entered are applied to this drive.
directory	Specifies the directory that is activated for command operations.
/MD *path*	Creates a directory, where *path* is the name of the new directory.
/DD *path*	Deletes the *path* directory and all contained files.
/RV *name*	Renames the drive volume to the specified *name*.
/RN *oldname newname*	Renames *oldname* directory to *newname*. Enter the entire path name for the old directory, but just the new name for the new directory.
/PG *prunepath graftpath*	Moves *prunepath* directory to *graftpath*. Enter the entire path name for both directories.
/MA *path* HSRA	Changes the attributes of the *path* directory. Enter the entire path name and specify the attributes you want to activate. Any attributes not specified are cleared.

/R	Rereads the directory tree for the current drive.

• **EXAMPLE** The following command deletes the \WORK\TEMP directory and all the files contained within it. Other subdirectories of the \WORK directory are unchanged.

DM DD \WORK\TEMP

See Also *Directory Maintenance, Add A Directory, Delete A Directory, Modify Attributes, Prune And Graft,* and *Rename A Directory* (Part 1)

DISKFIX

The DiskFix utility finds and fixes most disk problems and recovers data lost because of these problems. DiskFix is also useful as a tool for preventive maintenance.

Warning If you are experiencing disk problems and have not installed PC Tools, run DiskFix from a floppy disk. Copying the program onto the problem disk can overwrite data you may be able to recover otherwise.

If your computer does not boot when you turn it on, insert a floppy disk containing DOS (such as the recovery disk you made during installation) and reboot.

Memory-resident software, especially disk-caching programs other than PC-Cache, can conflict with DiskFix. For best results, remove all memory-resident programs other than the mouse driver and the PC Tools programs before running DiskFix.

To Start DiskFix

1. At the DOS prompt, enter the command

   DISKFIX

A warning message appears, reminding you to remove memory-resident programs.

2. Choose Cancel to quit and remove memory-resident programs, or choose **OK** to continue. DiskFix analyzes the partition tables and boot sectors of your hard disks. If there are problems, a dialog box appears giving you the option to repair the problems or quit. When all partition and boot information is valid, the main menu appears.

• **OPTIONS** The DiskFix main menu gives you six options:

Repair A Disk finds and fixes corrupted disk areas, including damaged partition tables and boot sectors, and errors in file structures, such as cross-linked files, lost cluster chains, and invalid directory entries. This option should be your first choice whenever you have problems reading data or accessing drives.

Surface Scan reads and writes data patterns on each disk cluster to locate damaged sectors. Once they are located, you can choose to remove damaged sectors from use and move data from those sectors to a safe location. Use this option regularly as a preventive maintenance tool.

Revitalize A Disk performs a nondestructive, low-level format of your disk. At the same time, it analyzes the media surface for the purpose of determining, and allowing you to select, the most efficient interleave factor for your drive. Use this option when experiencing problems that Repair A Disk and Surface Scan have been unable to fix, or if you encounter frequent read/write errors.

Undo A DiskFix Repair restores your disk to the condition it was in prior to running DiskFix. To invoke this command, you must have saved the original disk information to a floppy disk before performing the fix.

Configure Options sets testing and repair options according to your specifications.

Advice displays a menu of DOS error messages and common disk problems, and recommends corrective actions.

To Analyze and Repair a Disk

1. From the DiskFix main menu, choose **R**epair A Disk. The Drive Selection box appears.
2. Select the drive you want to repair, and choose **OK**. DiskFix runs through a series of analyses and tests; its progress is displayed on the Repair Drive screen.
3. If errors are found, a dialog box appears. Choose **R**epair, or follow the instructions and choose the appropriate command.
4. The first time a disk is repaired, a dialog box appears asking whether you want to save the current information. This allows you to undo the repair later. Select the drive to which you want to copy the current information, then choose **OK**.
5. A dialog box displays the progress of the repair operation. If lost clusters are found, you are given the following options:

   Save copies lost clusters to your root directory and names them PCT*nnnnn*.FIX, where *nnnnn* represents the sequential numbers of recovered clusters. If the lost cluster was a directory, the directory is renamed LOST*nnn*, and all its original files remain intact.

   Delete removes lost clusters. Use this option only if you are absolutely sure you don't need the data in these clusters.

   Ignore does nothing to the lost clusters. They remain allocated but are not available for use by your system.
6. When analyses and repairs are complete, a prompt is displayed asking whether you want a report of the results. Choose **OK** or **S**kip.
7. If you elect to generate a report of your results, choose **P**rinter to send the report to LPT1 (parallel port). Choose **F**ile to write the report to a text file in the DiskFix directory. The report file is named DISKFIX.RPT or another name you specify.

To Scan the Surface of a Disk

1. From the main DiskFix menu, choose **S**urface Scan. The Drive Selection box appears.
2. Select the drive you want to scan and choose **OK**.
3. Choose one of the following options:

   Read/Write Only reads and writes the entire drive and repairs problems, if possible. Use this option when scanning for preventive maintenance. It takes the least time to run but does not scan as thoroughly as pattern tests.

   Minimum Pattern Testing reads and writes 20 patterns and can detect flaws not found without pattern testing. Always use a pattern test if you are having read/write problems. Choose this option to perform the quickest but least thorough scan.

   Average Pattern Testing reads and writes 40 patterns. Use this option when you need to ensure the integrity of your disk but cannot take the time to do a Maximum scan.

   Maximum Pattern Testing reads and writes 80 patterns, the most thorough scan available. Use this option whenever time permits, the first time you run DiskFix, or when other options fail to correct problems.
4. Choose **OK** to continue. A drive map appears displaying the progress of the scan. You may choose **C**ancel at any time to interrupt the scan. If you do, choose **C**ontinue to resume the scan or **C**ancel again to return to the main menu.
5. When the scan is complete, a dialog box asks you whether you want a log report of the results. Choose **OK** to generate a report. Then choose **P**rinter to send the report to the LPT1 port or **F**ile to create a disk file of the report. The report file is written to the root directory and named DISKFIX.LOG unless you specify otherwise. Choose **S**kip to return to the main menu without generating a report.

To Revitalize a Disk

1. From the main DiskFix menu, choose Revitalize A Disk. The Drive Selection box appears.

2. Select the drive you want to revitalize and choose **O**K.
3. The program automatically runs through three types of tests: System Integrity, Timing Characteristics, and Physical Parameters. As each test is completed, choose **O**K to continue or Cancel to return to the main menu.
4. The program has now determined whether your disk can be low-level formatted. If it can, the program automatically runs the interleave test. This test determines the optimum ratio at which data can be read from your disk. Upon completion of this test, choose **F**astest to choose the recommended (highlighted) level. Or use the arrow keys or mouse to select another ratio, then choose **S**elected. Choose **O**K to save your changes, or choose **C**ancel to return to the main menu without saving.
5. The Pattern Testing dialog box appears. Choose an option. See step 3 of "To Scan the Surface of a Disk" to determine which option to choose.
6. Revitalization begins. A disk map appears displaying the progress of the operation. As the disk is revitalized, a log file is created describing defects and repairs. When the revitalization is finished, a dialog box asks you whether you want a log report of the results. Choose **O**K to generate a report. Then choose **P**rinter to send the report to the LPT1 port or **F**ile to create a disk file of the report. The report file is written to the root directory and named DISKFIX.LOG unless you specify otherwise. Choose **S**kip to return to the main menu without generating a report.

To Undo a DiskFix Repair

1. From the DiskFix main menu, choose **U**ndo A DiskFix Repair. The Drive Selection box appears.
2. Select the drive on which you saved the original disk information.
3. Choose **O**K. Your drive is restored to its "unfixed" state, and the main menu appears.

To Configure DiskFix Options

1. From the DiskFix main menu, choose Configure Options.
2. Choose one or more of the following options:

   Test Partition Information tests the partition information and boot sector every time you load DiskFix (the default is On).

   Check Boot Sector for Viruses searches the boot sector for viruses and displays a message if any are found (the default is On). This option can only be turned on if Test Partition Information is also on.

   Look For Mirror File searches for a Mirror file and compares it to the file allocation tables (FATs) for assistance in determining which FAT has fewer errors (the default is On).

   Use Custom Error Messages allows you to create custom error messages to replace all DiskFix error messages and prevents repairs from being made until the default messages are reset. You can use this option, for example, to prevent employees or inexperienced users from making repairs on their own. Instead of a repair message, you can substitute a message such as "Error Detected - Notify Supervisor Immediately!"

   Use BIOS Surface Scan performs a low-level scan. This is a more thorough, although slower, option.
3. To create custom error messages, choose Edit Custom Message. A text panel appears. Enter or edit the message as desired. Then choose OK to return to the previous window.
4. Choose OK to save your changes, or choose Cancel to return to the main menu without saving.

To Load DiskFix from DOS or a Batch File

Enter a command line in the following format at the DOS prompt or in your batch file:

DISKFIX *drive /options*

where *drive* is the drive to be repaired (the default is the current drive), and one or more of the following options is also included:

/TEST runs Repair A Disk on the specified drive, using options selected from DiskFix.

/SCAN runs Surface Scan on the specified drive, using the Read/Write Only option and other options selected from DiskFix.

/RO:*filename* generates a DiskFix report and overwrites the existing report, if any, when used with /TEST or /SCAN (uses the default unless another *filename* is specified).

/RA:*filename* appends the DiskFix report to the existing report when used with /TEST or /SCAN (uses the default unless another *filename* is specified).

/HCACHE is needed for systems with Hardcache cards.

/HCARD is needed for systems with HardCard cards.

• **NOTES** The default file names for DiskFix log reports are DISKFIX.RPT for Repair A Disk and DISKFIX.LOG for Surface Scan.

Windows users can use CP Scheduler to run DiskFix analyses at regular intervals to maintain optimum hard-drive performance.

FILEFIND

The FileFind utility allows you to locate one or more files according to selected specifications. You can specify search targets that are broad or narrow, depending on your requirements. You can locate files by name; with specified text strings within files; by date, size, and attributes; within user-defined groups; and with matching file names, sizes, or dates.

To Run FileFind from DOS or a Batch File

Enter a command line in the following format at the DOS prompt or within your batch file:

FF *drive filename searchtext /options*

• OPTIONS Use the following options when entering a FileFind command line:

drive	Specifies the drive to be searched.
filename	Designates the file specifications to be used as search targets. Use the DOS wildcards (* and ?), and enclose multiple specifications in quotation marks, separated by spaces.
searchtext	Specifies a text string to be used to locate files. Use the DOS wildcards (* and ?), and if your text string contains spaces, enclose the entire string in quotation marks.
/ALL	Searches all drives for files.
/CB	Searches the current directory and any subdirectories below it on the tree.
/CO	Searches only the current directory.
/CS	Designates a case-sensitive search.
/WW	Restricts a text search to whole words only. For example, if you enter *form* as a search string and turn on the /WW option, strings such as *format* and *forming* are ignored.
/A+ or /A–	Turns the archive attribute of located files on or off.
/H+ or /H–	Turns the hidden attribute of located files on or off.
/R+ or /R–	Turns the read-only attribute of located files on or off.
/S+ or /S–	Turns the system attribute of located files on or off.

/CLEAR	Turns off all attributes of located files.
/CURRENT	Sets time and date of located files to current system settings.
/D*mm-dd-yy*	Sets the date of located files to *month-day-year.*
/T*hh:mm*	Sets the time of located files to *hour:minutes.*
/F:*filename*	Creates a file (*filename*) listing all located files.

• **NOTE** The Locate command on the File menu in PC Shell calls the FileFind utility. For a detailed explanation of locating files by using FileFind menu structures and dialog boxes, see the Locate entry in Part 1.

See Also *Locate* (Part 1)

FILE FIX

The File Fix utility can recover damaged files created with Lotus 1-2-3 (versions 1 through 3), Symphony (version 1), dBASE (versions II, III, III PLUS, and IV), and many programs, such as Clipper and FoxPro, that use the dBASE file format.

To Load File Fix

1. At the DOS prompt, enter the command

   FILEFIX

   The main File Fix window appears.
2. Choose **D**base, **L**otus 1-2-3, or **S**ymphony.

To Recover a Spreadsheet File

1. Select the file you want to recover from the Files, Directories, and Drives lists in the Select File To Fix dialog box.

2. Choose **OK** to continue.
3. Enter a path and file name for the recovered file in the Repair To field, or accept the default.
4. Choose from the following options in the Repair Options dialog box:

   Recover All Data attempts to recover all data in the damaged file. Use this option first.

   Recover Cell Data Only recovers file data but not the formatting information. Use this option if you cannot open a file recovered with the Recover All Data option.

   File Is Password Protected decrypts the password-encrypted file and recovers data. Because an encryption is applied to these files, they might not be fully recovered.
5. Choose **OK** to continue.
6. If you are recovering a password-encrypted file, enter the password for the file. Then choose **OK**. The recovery process begins.
7. A screen display tracks the progress of the operation. Choose **OK** when it is finished.
8. A dialog box appears, asking whether you want to view the recovered file. Choose **OK** or **C**ancel.
9. Another dialog box appears, asking whether you want a report of the recovery. Choose **OK** to generate the report, or choose **C**ancel to return to the main window.
10. If you are generating a report, choose Report To **P**rinter to send the report to the LPT1 printer. Choose Report To **F**ile to save the report as a text file. The report is given the name of the recovered file with a .RPT extension, unless you specify otherwise.

Warning Do not delete original files before you have verified that the recovered files can be opened by the appropriate program. To open a recovered file, you must change the .FIX extension to .WKS, .WRK, .WK1, or .WR1, depending on the spreadsheet program.

• NOTES When you view a recovered file, the following highlighted symbols indicate the type of damage and what information you might need to reenter:

L The cell contained a label, but the data could not be recovered.

F The cell contained a formula, but the data could not be recovered.

N The cell contained a number, but the data could not be recovered.

A blank cell indicates that no information about the cell could be recovered.

For Lotus 1-2-3 and Symphony files, File Fix repairs the following types of problems:

- Invalid cell entries
- Invalid version number
- Damaged format
- Damage to global settings
- Damage to password-encrypted files
- Damaged formula cells and recalculation sequences

For dBASE files, File Fix repairs these problems:

- Damaged file headers
- Zapped files
- Record frame errors
- Embedded end-of-file (EOF) characters
- Illegal characters

To Recover a Database File

1. Select the file you want to recover from the Files, Directories, and Drives lists in the Select File To Fix dialog box.
2. Choose **OK** to continue.

3. Enter a path and file name for the recovered file in the Repair To field, or accept the default.

4. Choose from the following options in the Repair Options dialog box:

   Automatic Recovery recovers the file without further input. Always choose this option first.

   Display Damaged Records Before Fixing displays damaged records individually before repairs are made. Use this option if Automatic Recovery is unsuccessful.

   Display Each Record displays every file record. This option gives you the opportunity to reject records that File Fix does not. Use this option after you've tried the previous two options and still get "garbage" records.

   Check Data Alignment evaluates data alignment as the file is being repaired. Always use this option, unless you are certain the file contains only a few "garbage" characters.

   Check For Binary And Graphics Characters checks the file for special characters and replaces them with spaces unless you choose one of the display options above. Always choose this option unless you know the file contains valid graphics characters.

5. Choose **O**K to continue. The Bookkeeping Errors dialog box appears describing problems, if any, found in the record structure.

6. Choose **O**K to continue. Choose **R**eview to evaluate or modify the record structure (see "To Repair the Record Structure" below). The recovery process begins.

7. A screen display tracks the progress of the operation. Choose **O**K when it is finished.

8. A dialog box appears, asking whether you want to view the recovered file. Choose **O**K or **C**ancel.

9. Another dialog box appears, asking whether you want a report of the recovery. Choose **O**K to generate the report, or choose **C**ancel to return to the main window.

10. If you are generating a report, choose Report To **P**rinter to send the report to the LPT1 printer. Choose Report To **F**ile to save the report as a text file. The report is given the name of the recovered file with a .RPT extension, unless you specify otherwise.

Warning Do not delete original files before you know that the recovered files can be opened by the appropriate program. To open a recovered file, you must change the .FIX extension to .DBF or another extension appropriate to the database program.

• OPTIONS If you choose either of the nonautomatic recovery methods, you are given the following options when the program stops at a record:

Accept includes the record in the recovered file.

Reject excludes the record from the recovered file.

Mode displays the Repair Options dialog box and lets you switch recovery methods at any point in the recovery.

Cancel pauses the recovery and gives you options for resuming the operation, stopping at the current record, or canceling the entire operation.

To Repair the Record Structure

1. From the Bookkeeping Errors dialog box, choose **E**dit Existing Structure if no other file with the same structure exists, or choose **I**mport The Correct Structure From Another dBase File if you have another, undamaged dBASE file with the same record structure, such as a backup file or a prior version.

2. The next step depends on which option you chose in step 2:

    - If you chose the Import option, the Import File Structure dialog box appears. Select the file with the structure you want to import, then choose **OK**.

- If you chose the Edit Existing Structure option, the Adjust Starting Position dialog box appears. Use the arrow keys or the mouse to move the first character of data in the first record so that it is positioned in the upper-left corner of the text window. Then choose **O**K.

The Adjust Record Size dialog box appears. The first character of each record should be aligned at the left of the text window, and all record fields should be aligned in neat columns.

3. Use the arrow keys or click the arrow buttons to align records properly. Then choose **O**K. The Edit Record Structure dialog box appears.
4. In each field, the data should line up with the field names. If not, choose the field name and use the arrow keys or click the arrow buttons to adjust its width until it is properly aligned. Choose **A**dd or **D**elete to insert or remove fields. If you choose Add, enter field name, type, width, and decimals in the appropriate boxes.
5. When you are finished editing fields, choose **O**K.
6. Choose **R**evise if you get an error message. Repeat this procedure until you see no error messages.

KILL

The Kill utility removes the following PC Tools memory-resident programs: PC Shell, Desktop, Backtalk, CPSCHED, and DeskConnect.

To Remove Memory-Resident PC Tools Programs

At the DOS prompt, enter the command

KILL

Messages are displayed listing the programs that have been removed from memory.

LAUNCHER FOR WINDOWS

The Central Point Launcher for Windows utility allows you to run programs from any Windows application. Using Launcher, you do not have to return to the Program Manager window every time you want to run another program. When activated, a cascading Launcher submenu is available from the Control menu of any application window.

To Run Programs by Using Launcher

1. Click on the Control-menu box (in the upper-right corner) of any application window.
2. Choose CP **L**auncher. The cascading Launcher submenu appears.
3. Choose a listed program to launch that program, or choose **R**un. A dialog box appears that lists program files and directories. Enter the name of the file (including the path) that you want to run. Or move through the Files and Directories lists to select a program file. Then choose **OK** to launch the selected program.

To Configure the Launcher Menu

1. Choose **C**onfigure from the Launcher menu. The Configure Launcher dialog box appears.

2. To add an item to the Launcher submenu, choose **N**ew. All text boxes are cleared. Enter a name for the new **M**enu Item, an executable **L**aunch Command, and an **I**nitial Directory, if desired. The initial directory is activated when you load the program by using Launcher.
3. To edit an item, select the item from the **C**urrent Menu Items window. Move to the text box you want to change, and edit entries as desired.
4. Choose **D**elete to remove the current entry.
5. When you have finished configuring menu items, choose **S**ave to save your changes. Choose **OK** to return to the previous application window.

• NOTE The PC Tools Install program automatically installs Launcher in your Windows environment.

MEMORY INFORMATION

The Memory Information (MI) utility displays a summary report of your computer's memory usage.

To Evaluate Your Computer's Memory Usage

At the DOS prompt, enter the command in the following format:

MI */options*

• OPTIONS The following command-line options display memory information as needed:

/A Shows all memory blocks

/N	Disables the automatic pause when the screen is full
/Q	Displays a quick summary but gives no information about individual memory-resident programs
/F	Hides unprintable characters
/V	Lists the hooked vectors linked with memory blocks
/?	Displays a help screen of MI command-line options

MIRROR

The Mirror utility ensures recovery of the data (using Unformat) from an accidentally formatted hard disk. Mirror also improves data recoverability when you use DiskFix to repair disk damage. Mirror saves a copy of your file allocation table (FAT) and the root directory of your hard disk.

To Run Mirror from DOS or a Batch File

Enter the following command line at the DOS prompt or within a batch file, such as your AUTOEXEC.BAT file:

MIRROR *drive /options*

• **OPTIONS** Use the following command-line options to run the Mirror utility:

drive	Specifies a drive for Mirror to protect (you can specify multiple drives, separated with spaces)
/1	Specifies that Mirror only save the latest file allocation table (FAT) and directory information (saves some space on your hard disk but reduces your chances for data recovery)

/PARTN	Saves a copy of your partition table, boot record, and CMOS information on a floppy disk
/NOCMOS	Used with /PARTN, saves the partition table and boot record but omits CMOS information
/?	Displays a help screen with Mirror command-line options

• NOTE Unless specified, Mirror saves two copies of your system information. The latest version is saved in a file named MIRROR.FIL. The previous version is saved in a file named MIRROR.BAK. Saving two versions provides an extra layer of protection.

See Also *Unformat*

PARK

The Park utility moves the read/write heads of your hard disk to a safe location, reducing the chances that they will damage your disk when you move your computer.

TO PARK YOUR DISK HEADS

At the DOS prompt, enter the command

PARK

• NOTE There are no command-line options available with the Park utility.

PC-CACHE

The PC-Cache utility speeds up your hard drive's performance by acting as a mediator between your hard disk and your applications. Frequently needed data is moved into a reserved memory cache where it can be accessed quickly. Because PC-Cache reduces the number of mechanical hard-disk accesses, your programs run significantly faster.

To Install PC-Cache

Enter the following command line at the DOS prompt or within a batch file, such as your AUTOEXEC.BAT file:

PC-CACHE */options*

The program is loaded, and a status window is displayed.

Warning Do not use PC-Cache simultaneously with other caching programs. For example, if you are using Windows, do not use PC-Cache and SMARTDRIVE.SYS—unpredictable results may occur.

• **OPTIONS** Use the following command-line options when loading PC-Cache:

/EXTSTART=*n*K	Loads PC-Cache at a specified address in extended memory. The address, *n*K, must be greater than 1024K (1MB).
/FLUSH	Empties the cache and writes its contents to disk.
/I*drive*	Excludes the specified drive from cache operations. Use this option to exclude RAM disks and Bernoulli boxes.

/NOBATCH	Specifies, for extended memory caches only, that only one sector of data is transferred at a time. This option may be needed when using communications software at very high baud rates.
/PAUSE	Pauses the program when the status window is displayed. Use this option when you load PC-Cache from your AUTOEXEC.BAT file and want to see the status window before you proceed.
/QUIET	Disables the status window display.
/SIZEXP=*nnnn*	Designates the amount (*nnnn*) of expanded memory allocated to PC-Cache. The minimum setting is 32K. The default setting is 256K.
/SIZEXT=*nnnn*	Designates the amount (*nnnn*) of extended memory allocated to PC-Cache. The minimum setting is 8K. The default setting is 256K.
/SIZEXT*=*nnnn*	Uses the BIOS to access a cache in extended memory. Use this option if PC-Cache fails to load with the /SIZEXT=*nnnn* option.
/UNLOAD	Removes PC-Cache from memory.
/WIN	Instructs PC-Cache to adjust its size automatically when Windows is loaded.
/WRITE=ON or /WRITE=OFF	Turns on or off the writing of data to disk through PC-Cache.
/?	Displays a help screen with PC-Cache command-line options.

• **NOTES** You must install PC-Cache after Mirror but before any other memory-resident programs.

The PC Tools Install program can automatically configure and insert a PC-Cache command line in your AUTOEXEC.BAT file.

PC-Cache can be used with any type of memory (conventional, expanded, and extended) and can support multiple hard drives.

PC CONFIG

The PC Config utility allows you to configure the color, display, mouse, and keyboard elements of the PC Tools programs.

To Load PC Config

1. At the DOS prompt, enter the command

   PCCONFIG

   The program is loaded, and the main PC Config window appears.
2. Choose one of the following elements to configure:

   Color changes the colors used in display screens, message windows, and dialog boxes.

   Display sets display modes.

   Mouse sets mouse modes and speed.

   Keyboard sets keyboard repeat rate and delay.
3. After you have made all your changes, choose Exit to quit.

To Change Screen Colors

Use the Color Options window to change colors displayed in different parts and for different elements of the screen. For example, you can change the color of dialog boxes and the text displayed in them, or you can create an entirely new color scheme for PC Tools. In addition, PC Tools comes with several color schemes that you can implement easily. (The Color Options menu is also available using the Colors command from PC Shell.)

To Configure Your Display

From the Display Options menu, choose from the following options:

Text Mode uses only regular characters to display screen features. You see parentheses and brackets instead of circles and boxes.

Graphics Mode uses special graphics characters to display screen features. You see circles and boxes instead of parentheses and brackets. This option is available only with VGA and EGA monitors.

Fast Video On CGA sets a faster screen retrace speed for CGA monitors. If this option is on, the screen scrolls faster, but may display "snow" or flickering.

25 Lines sets a 25-line screen (the default).

28 Lines sets a 28-line screen (available only with VGA monitors).

43 Lines sets a 43-line screen (available only with EGA monitors).

50 Lines sets a 50-line screen (available only with VGA monitors).

To Configure Your Mouse

From the Mouse Options dialog box, choose from the following options:

Fast Mouse Reset sets your mouse for optimum operation. Turn this option off if your mouse doesn't work properly, especially when using a PS/2-type mouse after running Windows 3.0.

Left Handed Mouse exchanges the left and right mouse button functions so that the mouse can be used on the left side of the keyboard.

Disable Mouse disables your mouse for PC Tools programs. Use this option if your mouse driver is incompatible with PC Tools.

Graphics Mouse displays the mouse as an arrow when turned on and as a solid block when turned off (available only with VGA monitors).

Speed sets the rate of movement for your mouse. The higher the setting, the more the cursor moves across the screen in response to the movement of the mouse on your desktop.

To Configure Keyboard Options

From the Keyboard Options dialog box, choose from the following options:

Enable Keyboard Speed activates the keyboard rate and delay settings you specify. If this option is off, your rate and delay settings are ignored.

Rate sets the speed at which a keystroke is repeated when you hold down a key. The higher the number, the faster the repeat rate.

Delay sets the amount of time a key must be held down before it begins to repeat. The higher the number, the longer the delay.

PC FORMAT

PC Format replaces the DOS Format utility. PC Format is faster, easier to use, and safer than DOS Format. It includes many features that greatly increase your chances of recovering data if a disk containing data is accidentally formatted. You can use PC Format to format floppy disks, hard disks, and Bernoulli boxes.

To Load PC Format

1. At the DOS prompt, enter the command

   PCFORMAT

   The program is loaded, and the Drive Selection dialog box appears.

2. Select the drive you want to format, then choose **OK**. The Select Format Options dialog box appears.

3. Choose the formatting method you want to use:

   Safe Format formats the disk so that you can recover the contents, if necessary, using Unformat.

   Quick Format erases the root directory and file allocation table (FAT) but does not erase data or check media sectors. Use this option when formatting Bernoulli boxes, RAM disks, and previously formatted disks.

   Full Format reads, formats, and rewrites data (if any) to each track. The root directory and FAT are cleared. This option may repair a disk with marginal sector IDs. It is not available for hard disks.

   Destructive Format formats a disk and erases its entire contents. A disk formatted with this option cannot be recovered. Use this option for security purposes, such as when you are reusing a floppy disk that previously contained confidential information. This option is not available for hard disks.

4. Choose **I**nstall System Files to include the operating system on your formatted disk. This option creates a bootable disk.

5. Choose Save **M**irror Info if you have used Mirror previously on the disk you want to format and you want to preserve that information. This option increases your chances of recovering data on the disk.

6. Choose **L**abel and enter a name for the disk (11 characters maximum), if desired.

7. Choose the capacity of the disk to be formatted (see "Warning" below). Choose **OK**.

8. If there are files on the disk, they are listed in a new dialog box and you are prompted to confirm the format. Choose **OK** to continue formatting, or choose **C**ancel to return to the Select Format Options dialog box.

9. After formatting is complete, the Select Format Options dialog box appears. Repeat steps 3 through 8, or choose Cancel to quit.

10. To exit PC Format, choose Exit then **OK**.

Warning Make sure you select the proper capacity for the disk you are formatting. Disks that are formatted improperly may not be recoverable.

Once you save files on a disk, you lose data in the sectors in which those files are written. These sectors cannot be recovered.

The Unformat program is designed to recover disks that have been formatted. However, it is not foolproof. When formatting disks, use extreme caution not to format disks containing important files. Make backups of disks and files you may need later.

• OPTIONS Use the following command-line options to bypass the program dialog boxes and specify formatting options:

drive	Specifies the drive to be formatted.
/1	Specifies a single-sided format.
/4	Specifies a 360K format in a high-capacity drive. Use this option to format a 360K disk in a 1.2MB disk drive. A disk formatted in this way may not be readable in a 360K drive.
/8	Specifies eight sectors per track, for use with versions of DOS prior to DOS 2.0.
/DESTROY	Specifies a destructive format; all data are erased.
/F	Specifies a full format; all data are erased.
/F:*n*K	Designates disk capacity (floppy drives only). Valid entries are 160, 180, 320, 360, 720, 1200, 1400, and 2880 (DOS 5 only).
/N:*n*	Sets the number of sectors per track. Valid entries are 8, 9, 15, and 36.

/P	Prints the screen information to the LPT1 printer.
/Q	Specifies a quick format.
/R	Specifies a full format; data are not erased.
/S	Creates a bootable disk by copying the operating system onto it.
/TEST	Simulates a format without writing to the disk. Use this option to familiarize yourself with format messages and prompts.
/V	Displays a prompt asking you to enter a volume label.
/V:*label*	Adds the specified volume *label* to the disk.
/?	Displays a help screen with PC Format command-line options.

• **NOTES** When you install PC Tools, you are given the option of renaming the DOS FORMAT command to FORMAT!. If you choose this option, Install creates a FORMAT batch command so that you can load PC FORMAT simply by entering FORMAT at the DOS PROMPT.

When you use PC Format on a floppy disk, the program reads the disk first to determine whether it contains data. If so, the data is not overwritten (unlike the DOS Format utility). The file allocation table (FAT) and the first characters of all file names in the root directory are cleared. The first characters of file names are stored in a special area in the root directory. The disk can be restored by using the Rebuild utility, provided it has not been overwritten.

When you use PC Format on a hard disk, the FAT and the first characters of all file names in the root directory are cleared and stored in a special area in the root directory. The disk can be restored by using the Unformat utility, provided it has not been overwritten.

See Also *Make Disk Bootable* and *Format A Data Disk* (Part 1)

PC SECURE

The PC Secure utility protects confidential data by encrypting, or scrambling, the contents of files. They cannot be read until they are decrypted. PC Secure meets U.S. Department of Defense standards for file security. You can use PC Secure to encrypt and decrypt data files (except for compressed or archived files), network files, and applications.

To Load PC Secure

1. At the DOS prompt, enter the command

   PCSECURE

   The program is loaded. The first time you load the program, you are prompted to create a master key. The master key is used to override passwords for encrypted files (in advanced mode).

2. Enter the master key password in the appropriate field. Press F9 to enter a master key with hexadecimal values.

3. Enter the master key again to verify it. The main PC Secure window appears.

Warning Do not lose or forget your master key or encryption passwords. For maximum security, do not use passwords that can be guessed easily, such as keys based on your name, initials, or birth date.

To Encrypt a File

1. Pull down the **F**ile menu.
2. Choose **E**ncrypt File. The File Selection dialog box appears.
3. In the Filename text box, enter the name of the file you want to encrypt. Or use the arrow keys or the mouse to select the file from the Files, Directories, and Drives lists.
4. Enter a password for the selected file, and press Enter.

5. Enter the password again for verification, and press Enter. A summary of the encryption operation is displayed.
6. Choose **O**K to return to the PC Secure window.

To Decrypt a File

1. Pull down the File menu.
2. Choose **D**ecrypt File. The File Selection dialog box appears.
3. In the Filename text box, enter the name of the encrypted file you want to decrypt. Or use the arrow keys or the mouse to select the file from the Files, Directories, and Drives lists.
4. Enter the password used to encrypt the selected file, and press Enter.
5. Enter the password again for verification, and press Enter. A summary of the decryption operation is displayed.
6. Choose **O**K to return to the PC Secure window.

To Configure PC Secure

1. Pull down the **O**ptions menu.
2. Choose from the following options:

   Full DES Encryption applies a full encryption to the file by using the complete Data Encryption Scheme (DES) algorithm. This option provides the greatest security.

   Quick Encryption applies an abbreviated encryption to the file. It runs twice as fast as a full encryption but is slightly less secure.

   Compression compresses files from 25 percent to 60 percent of their original size. You can use this option with no perceptible loss of speed.

   One Key encrypts a group of files using the same password. During encryption and decryption sessions, you are prompted only once for the password.

Hidden hides encrypted files from the DOS DIR command. The file is still displayed in PC Shell.

Read-Only designates the file as read-only so that it cannot be deleted accidentally.

Delete Original File replaces the original file with the encrypted file. If this option is turned off, the encrypted file is renamed with an .SEC extension and the original file is retained.

Expert Mode disables the master key. When Expert Mode is on, the master key is not applied to encrypted files. This means that you cannot use the master key you created in your first PC Secure session to decrypt the file if you lose the encryption password.

To Run PC Secure Automatically or from a Batch File

Enter a command line in the following format at the DOS prompt or within a batch file:

PCSECURE */options filename* **or** *filespec*

- **OPTIONS** Use the following command-line options:

/C	Turns the compression option off for encryption operations
/G	Deletes original files according to DOD (U.S. Department of Defense) specifications
/M	Allows files to be encrypted multiple times, requiring multiple passwords that must be entered in sequence for decryption
/S	Turns off the status window (only error messages are displayed)
/VIDEO	Displays a help screen with display and mouse options that can be entered from the command line
/F	Applies a Full DES Encryption to the files

/Q	Applies a Quick Encryption to the files
/D	Decrypts files
/K*key*	Assigns *key* as the password for files (a space ends the key)
/P	Displays a prompt for the password to be entered, for greater security
filename	Designates the name of the file to be encrypted or decrypted; you can enter multiple file names, separated by spaces
filespec	Designates a group of files to be encrypted or decrypted according to file specifications; use DOS wildcards (* or ?) and separate multiple specifications with spaces

See Also *Decrypt File*, *Encrypt File*, and *Settings* (Part 1)

REBUILD

The Rebuild utility allows you to restore your hard disk if it is damaged. Rebuild uses information stored on your recovery disk (created by the Install program), including the PARTNSAV.FIL file, which contains information about your hard drive's partition table, boot sector, and CMOS information.

To Restore the CMOS Information

1. Insert your recovery disk in the appropriate floppy drive.
2. Reboot your computer by pressing Ctrl-Alt-Del.
3. From the DOS prompt, enter the command

   REBUILD

4. Enter the letter of the floppy drive that has the recovery disk. The CMOS and partition table information stored on

your recovery disk are displayed. (Press Ctrl-S to pause scrolling.)

5. To restore the CMOS information, press C, then Enter.
6. When the restoration is complete, you are prompted to open the floppy-drive door. The program then automatically reboots your machine.

To Restore the Partition Table and Boot Sector

1. Insert your recovery disk in the appropriate floppy drive.
2. Reboot your computer by pressing Ctrl-Alt-Del.
3. From the DOS prompt, enter the command

   REBUILD

4. Enter the letter of the floppy drive that has the recovery disk. The CMOS and partition table information stored on your recovery disk are displayed. (Press Ctrl-S to pause scrolling.)
5. Select a partition to restore:
   - Choose **All** to restore partition tables for all hard drives on your system (this option only appears if you have more than one fixed disk).
   - Choose **1** through **8** to restore individual drives (fixed disks or hard drives).
6. Enter **YES** to confirm.
7. When the restoration is complete, you are prompted to open the floppy-drive door. The program then automatically reboots your machine.

• OPTIONS Use the following options from the DOS command line:

drive Specifies the drive containing the PARTNSAV.FIL file.

/ICHK	Ignores the checksum protocol and loads CMOS on the computer. The checksum characterizes the PARTNSAV data as belonging to a specific computer. Use this option to override the checksum.
/LIST	Lists partitions on the existing hard drive without changing data.
/N	Disables pausing at a full screen; used only with /LIST.
/TEST	Simulates the Rebuild process; the CMOS and partition table remain unchanged.

SWAPDT AND SWAPSH

The SWAPDT and SWAPSH utilities decrease the amount of conventional memory needed to load the Desktop Manager and PC Shell as memory-resident programs. SWAPDT loads the resident portion of the Desktop Manager into expanded (EMS) or extended (XMS) memory, or onto your hard disk. SWAPSH performs the same function for PC Shell. Install SWAPDT and SWAPSH after any disk-caching utilities. Install SWAPDT before the Desktop Manager and SWAPSH before PC Shell.

To Load SWAPDT or SWAPSH from DOS or a Batch File

Enter the following command line at the DOS prompt or within a batch file, such as your AUTOEXEC.BAT file:

SWAPDT */options*

or

SWAPSH */options*

• OPTIONS Use the following command-line options for SWAPDT and SWAPSH:

/N	Disables memory-resident mode and waits for a Desktop command
/U	Removes SWAPDT from memory
/D*path*	Specifies a path for the swapped files (the default is C:\)
/S*x*	Specifies the type of swap: *0* is automatic, *1* swaps to disk, *2* swaps to extended memory, and *3* swaps to expanded memory (the default is /S0)
/P*x*	Specifies the size of the pasting buffer for the Clipboard, where *x* is a number between 0 and 9, which represents the number of 256K increments making up the Clipboard buffer
/T*x*	Sets the speed of Clipboard pasting, where *x* is a number between 0 (slowest) and 3 (fastest)

You can also use these options to configure the hotkey for PC Shell:

/A	Selects the Alt key as the hotkey
/C	Selects the Ctrl key as the hotkey
/L	Selects the left Shift key as the hotkey
/R	Selects the right Shift key as the hotkey
/K*xx*	Defines *xx* as the hotkey, where *xx* is a hexadecimal value

• NOTES Use the Utilities command on the Desktop main menu to change the hotkey for the Desktop Manager.

The PC Tools Install program can configure your AUTOEXEC.BAT file to include the SWAPSH and SWAPDT utilities.

SYSTEM INFORMATION

The System Information (SI) utility displays information about the inner workings of your computer, such as memory allocation, disk-drive specifications, monitor specifications, and the CPU. It also allows you to view your AUTOEXEC.BAT and CONFIG.SYS files.

You can run the System Information utility from the DOS prompt and within batch files, or from the Special menu in PC Shell. See the System Info command in Part 1 for detailed procedures.

To Run System Information from DOS or a Batch File

At the DOS prompt or from within a batch file, enter the following command line:

SI */options*

- **OPTIONS** Use these command-line options:

/MEM	Loads the program and automatically displays the Memory Information window
/RPT	Prints the entire system information report to a disk file named SI.RPT
/DEMO	Displays in sequence several of the most important system information windows
/NOVID	Disables extended video checking
/?	Displays a help screen with command-line options

See Also *System Info* (Part 1)

TSR MANAGER FOR WINDOWS

The TSR Manager lets you access memory-resident PC Tools programs while working in Windows. Specifically, if VDefend, Commute, or Data Monitor are resident in memory, the messages they generate are displayed when Windows is running. You can also run Commute or run and configure Data Monitor from the TSR Manager dialog box.

To Run Commute from the TSR Manager

1. Click on the TSR Manager icon to open the TSR Manager dialog box.
2. Choose **C**ommute. A message window appears.
3. Choose **OK** to return to the TSR Manager dialog box.
4. Choose **R**un Commute to run the program. When you exit, you are returned to Windows.

To Configure and Run Data Monitor from the TSR Manager

1. Open the TSR Manager dialog box.
2. Choose **D**ata Monitor. A message window appears.
3. Choose Enable **D**irectory Lock or Enable **W**rite Protect if desired. Choose **OK** to return to the TSR Manager dialog box.
4. Choose **R**un Data Monitor to run the program. The program is loaded and allows you to configure Data Monitor options. All options, with the exceptions of Disk Light and Screen Blanker, are in effect when you return to Windows.

• **NOTE** The TSR Manager is installed automatically by the PC Tools Install program when the Install Windows Applications option is enabled.

See Also *Commute* and *Data Monitor*

UNDELETE

The Undelete utility recovers accidentally deleted files. It can be loaded from the DOS prompt or from the File menu in PC Shell. Use automatic undeletes when files are deleted with either Delete Sentry or Delete Tracker protection turned on. (See the Undelete entry in Part 1 for information on performing automatic undeletes.) Use advanced undeletes (described in this section) when deleted files are in Poor condition, have been deleted by DOS, or are in Good or Excellent condition but contain overwritten clusters.

To Undelete Files by Using Advanced Options

1. From the file list, select one or more deleted files to undelete.
2. Pull down the **F**ile menu.
3. Choose **A**dvanced Undelete.
4. Designate a recovery file by choosing one of these options:

   Manual Undelete recovers the file, using the original file name.

   Create A File lets you specify a path and file.

   Append To Existing File adds clusters to an existing file that you specify. This option is available only when the Show Existing Files option is selected from the Options menu.

   Rename Existing File lets you rename existing files so that you can recover a deleted file with the same name. This option is available only when the Show Existing Files option is selected from the Options menu.

5. If you chose Manual Undelete and the file was deleted with DOS, enter the first letter of the file name. If you chose any of the other options, enter a file name and choose **OK**.

The Manual Undelete window appears. Information about the selected file is displayed in the upper-left corner. In the List Of Added Clusters box, the Starting Cluster field shows the number of the first cluster in the file. The Clusters Needed field shows the number of clusters allocated to the file before it was deleted. The Clusters Added field tracks the number of clusters you add to the file. When you add clusters, they are listed in the scrollable window on the right.

To Add Deleted Clusters to the Recovery File

1. From the Manual Undelete dialog box, choose **Add Cluster**. The Cluster Options dialog box appears.
2. Choose from these options:

   Add All Clusters automatically writes all deleted clusters to the file.

   Add This Cluster adds clusters one at a time.

   View This Cluster opens the Cluster Viewer and displays the contents of the next cluster available. You can then choose **Add Cluster** or **Next Cluster**.

   Scan For Contents searches your disk's free clusters for the text string you specify.

   Enter Cluster # allows you to specify by number a cluster to add to the file. This option is useful if you know the approximate location on disk of the deleted file.

• OPTIONS You can also choose from the Manual Undelete dialog box the options that follow:

Skip Cluster ignores the current cluster and moves to the next one.

View File opens the file viewer and displays the contents of the recovery file. If the first cluster is recognizable, the file is displayed in its native format.

Update undeletes the file and updates the file allocation table (FAT) to include the recovered clusters.

In addition, the cluster list can be edited by using the options that follow:

Move allows you to reposition the current cluster.

Delete removes the current cluster from the list.

To Run Undelete from DOS or a Batch File

Enter a command line in this format:

UNDEL *drive filename /options*

- **OPTIONS** Use the command-line options that follow:

drive	Specifies the drive from which you want to recover data
filename	Specifies the path and file to be recovered (you can use the DOS wildcards * and ? to specify a group of files)
/ALL	Undeletes files regardless of delete method (the default)
/DOS	Undeletes only files deleted by DOS
/DT	Undeletes files by using Delete Tracker information
/LIST	Lists all deleted files available for recovery in the specified directory
/M	Undeletes DOS-deleted files by using information created by the Mirror utility
/NC	Disables the confirmation prompt when undeleting files
/NM	Undeletes DOS-deleted files without using Mirror information
/S	Undeletes files deleted with Delete Sentry protection
/?	Displays a help screen with command-line options

UNDELETE FOR WINDOWS

The Undelete for Windows utility allows you to restore deleted files from the Windows environment. Although the look of Undelete for Windows differs from the DOS version, the menus, dialog boxes, and command sequences are similar to those of the DOS version, with the following exceptions:

- The directory tree is not displayed automatically. To change directories, click on the Drive/Dir command button in the main window or pull down the **F**ile menu and choose Change **D**rive/Directory.
- The main menu includes command buttons for the following pull-down menu selections: Drive/Dir File Info and Find Deleted Files from the File menu, and Sort By from the Options menu.
- The Print command allows you to print the current file list.
- The Printer Setup command allows you to configure your printer from within Undelete.
- The Configure Delete Protection command from the Options menu allows you to enable Delete Sentry or Delete Tracker protection without leaving Undelete.
- Lost files (unallocated sectors) cannot be scanned.
- Files cannot be viewed.

• **NOTE** Use the step-by-step procedures for running the DOS version of Undelete to run Undelete for Windows.

See Also *Undelete*

UNFORMAT

The Unformat utility recovers data from accidentally formatted disks. For hard disks, Unformat rebuilds the file allocation table (FAT) and root directory by using Mirror information or, if the Mirror file is unavailable, from the data on the disk. For floppy disks, Unformat can recover data only if the disk was formatted with PC Format. DOS-formatted disks are unrecoverable. (Use Unformat to recover data lost by using the FORMAT, RECOVER, and DEL *.* commands.)

Warning Use Unformat immediately after an accidental format. If you continue to use the disk, data may be overwritten.

To Unformat a Disk

1. From the DOS prompt (in the PC Tools directory), enter the command

   UNFORMAT

   or

   UNFORMAT *drive*

2. If you do not enter a drive designation on the command line, the Drive Selection dialog box appears. Select the drive to unformat, then choose **O**K.

3. Unformat validates the drive and the Mirror Used? window appears. Choose **Y**es if the Mirror program was run on the disk or if you aren't sure and you want Unformat to search for the Mirror files. Choose **N**o if Mirror information is unavailable.

4. If there are any files in the root directory, a dialog box appears listing them. If you want to keep any of these files, choose Cancel, exit Unformat, and copy them to another disk. Choose **O**K to continue. Unformat begins recovering the disk.

5. If there are fragmented files on the disk, you are given these options:

   Delete deletes the current file. Use this option if you want to recover the entire file. Deleted fragmented files usually can be recovered entirely by using Undelete.

   Delete All deletes all fragmented files without further confirmation.

   Truncate recovers the first group of contiguous clusters in the file. In the absence of a Mirror file, Unformat can only identify the beginning of the file. Noncontiguous clusters are lost.

   Truncate All truncates all fragmented files without further confirmation.

6. When unformatting is finished, choose **Exit**. Reboot, if necessary.

If you need to reboot, do not reboot from the drive you want to recover. For example, if you accidentally format a disk in floppy-drive A, remove the disk from the drive and reboot the system from your hard drive. In this way you do not overwrite the Mirror file needed for recovery. (If you need to reboot from a floppy drive, use the recovery disk created by the PC Tools Install program.)

• NOTES Before you run Unformat, unload from memory any disk-caching programs other than PC-Cache.

Once unformatting is finished, it is good practice to verify your system and data:

- Run Repair A Disk in DiskFix to make sure there is no damage to the file allocation tables.
- Try to run your applications. If you cannot, the program files may have been fragmented and could not be recovered. If so, reinstall your programs from floppy disks.
- Open your data files. If they are corrupted, restore them from backup copies, or reenter lost information.

VDEFEND

The VDefend utility can protect your computer from over 500 viruses. When program files are loaded or copied, VDefend checks them for known viruses. In addition, VDefend prompts for confirmation anytime you attempt a low-level format, because this is how some viruses do their damage. You can run VDefend from either your AUTOEXEC.BAT or CONFIG.SYS file.

Tip Central Point updates VDefend regularly to maintain its virus-protection capabilities. To update your copy of VDefend, download the SIGNATURE.CPS file from the Central Point BBS or the Central Point Forum on CompuServe, and copy it to the directory where VDefend is installed.

To Run VDefend from AUTOEXEC.BAT

Enter the following line in your AUTOEXEC.BAT file:

VDEFEND

VDefend is automatically loaded as a memory-resident program every time you boot your machine.

When VDefend is run from the DOS prompt, a batch file, or AUTOEXEC.BAT, it can be removed from memory by entering

VDEFEND /U

at the DOS prompt.

To Run VDefend from CONFIG.SYS

Enter the following line in your CONFIG.SYS file:

DEVICE=VDEFEND.SYS

VDefend is loaded every time you boot.

• NOTE When VDefend is run from CONFIG.SYS, it is loaded before the command processor (COMMAND.COM) and consequently can check that file for viruses. It cannot, however, be unloaded from memory at the DOS prompt. To remove it, remove the command from your CONFIG.SYS file and reboot.

VIEW

The View utility displays file contents without starting a program. You can view word processing files, spreadsheet files, database files, graphics files, binary files, and archived files. Simply select a file, then activate the viewer. The program automatically chooses the proper viewer and displays the file approximately as it would appear in the program. (For procedures on using View, see the View File Contents command entry in Part 1.)

To Run View from the DOS Prompt

Enter a command line in the format

VIEW *filespec*

where *filespec* specifies a path and file or group of files to be viewed. Use the DOS wildcards (* and ?) to specify file groups.

• NOTE The View utility is used by many PC Tools utilities, including Undelete, File Fix, FileFind, PC Shell, and CP Backup. These utilities call View to allow you to see the contents of files you are manipulating.

See Also *View File Contents* (Part 1)

WIPE

The Wipe utility protects the confidentiality of your data by completely erasing it from disk. When you delete files, they are not really erased; only their directory entries are erased. The data they contain can be recovered by using Undelete. The Wipe utility deletes files, directories, or entire drives, and writes a user-definable character over the disk space containing them. (The Wipe utility conforms to Department of Defense standards for clearing data.)

Warning Once files have been wiped, they are cleared completely from storage. They cannot be recovered or read by any means. Give yourself room for error. If you want to maintain confidentiality but not lose files, make backup copies on floppy disks and store them securely. Use Delete to remove files for which confidentiality isn't required. Deleted files usually can be recovered by using Undelete.

To Load Wipe

1. At the DOS prompt, enter the command

   WIPE

   The main Wipe menu appears.

2. Choose one of these options:

   Files wipes one or more files you select.

   Disk wipes an entire disk.

   Configure allows you to choose Wipe options.

To Wipe Files from Disk

- From the main Wipe window, choose **F**ile. The File Options dialog box appears.

  Specify the files you want to wipe in the File Specification text box. Use DOS wildcards (* and ?) to represent a group of files. Choose Drive or Directory to change the current drive or directory.

3. Choose from the Wipe options that follow:

Confirm each file displays a confirmation message and prompt before each file is cleared.

Include subdirectories wipes files in subdirectories of the current directory that match the file specification.

Include hidden files clears hidden files that match the file specification.

Include read-only files clears read-only files that match the file specification.

Only modified files clears only files for which the archive attribute is set, indicating files have been changed since the last backup.

Only unmodified files clears files for which the archive attribute is off, indicating files have not been changed since the last backup.

Modified and unmodified files clears files regardless of the archive attribute.

Wipe files clears files from disk and overwrites them with the specified character (see "To Configure Wipe").

Clear only unused file space clears only the unused space associated with files, usually at the end of the clusters allocated to the file.

Delete files deletes files (removes directory entries). Unlike the DOS Delete command, this option allows you to delete hidden and read-only files.

Older than clears files meeting the file specification that were created before the date and time specified.

Equal to clears files meeting the file specification that were created at the date and time specified.

Younger than clears files meeting the file specification that were created after the date and time specified.

Any date/time clears all files meeting the file specification regardless of their date/time attribute.

4. When you have set the options you want, choose **O**K to continue.
5. If Confirm Each File is on, you are prompted before each file is wiped. Choose **S**kip to retain the current file and move to the next one. Choose **W**ipe to wipe the current file and move to the next one. A dialog box appears summarizing the operation.

To Wipe a Disk

1. From the main Wipe window, choose **D**isk. The Disk Options dialog box appears, with the current drive activated.
2. Choose Change **D**rive to select another drive.
3. Choose one of the Wipe disk options that follow:

   Wipe disk clears the entire disk.

   Clear only unused disk space clears only unallocated disk space. Existing files and directories remain intact.
4. Choose **O**K to continue, or choose **C**ancel to return to the Wipe main menu. Choose **W**ipe.
5. A message window summarizes the progress of the Wipe operation. Choose **S**top to interrupt.

To Configure Wipe

1. From the main Wipe window, choose Configure. The Configuration Options dialog box appears.
2. Choose from the options that follow:

   Fast wipe overwrites disk areas with the character you specify (the default is 0) and repeats the operations the number of times you specify (the default is 1).

   DOD wipe clears files according to U.S. Department of Defense standards. You can specify the number of times the operation is repeated (the default is 3) and the hexadecimal value of the overwrite character (the default is 246). The default settings meet DOD specifications.

3. To save the current configuration, choose **S**ave Config. Choose **OK** to continue with the options you set for the current session, or choose **C**ancel to return to the main menu without resetting options.

To Run Wipe from DOS or a Batch File

Enter a command line in the following format at the DOS prompt or from within a batch file:

WIPE *drive /options*

- **OPTIONS** Use the command-line options that follow:

drive	Specifies the drive for a disk wipe
/DELETE	Deletes files without wiping them
/DISK	Wipes an entire disk
/GOVT	Wipes files according to Department of Defense specifications
/HIDDEN	Includes hidden files meeting the file specification in the Wipe operation
/MODIFIED	Deletes or wipes only files modified since the last backup
/NONCONFIRM	Disables the confirmation message and prompt
/QUIET	Disables prompts and displays only the summary window
/READONLY	Includes read-only files meeting the file specification in the Wipe operation
/REP:*n*	Repeats the operation the specified number of times
/SUB	Includes subdirectories
/UNMODIFIED	Deletes or wipes only files not modified since the last backup
/UNUSED	Wipes only unused disk space

/VALUE:*n*	Uses the character represented by the hexadecimal value (*n*) as the overwrite character

See Also *Clear File* (Part 1)

Appendix

Data Recovery Guidelines

This appendix has guidelines for recovering data and preventing data loss.

If you have lost data, use the following list to determine which program to use (and where to look in this book) to attempt recovery:

Problem	See
You accidentally delete a file	Undelete (Part 3)
You accidentally format a disk	Unformat (Part 3)
You experience disk problems	DiskFix (Part 3)

The data recovery capabilities of PC Tools are most effective when used in conjunction with the following preventive techniques:

- Create a recovery disk. If you didn't create a recovery disk when you installed PC Tools, run PC Install again. The recovery disk stores the operating system, hard-drive partition table, CMOS information, and boot sector information. If your system crashes, you can use the recovery disk to restart your computer and to restore your hard drive.
- Run MIRROR from your AUTOEXEC.BAT file. The Mirror program saves one or two copies (depending on how you configure it) of your file allocation table (FAT) and can be used to recover lost files if your FAT is corrupted. By running MIRROR from your AUTOEXEC.BAT file, you create backups of your FAT each time you start your computer.
- Make regular backups of your hard disk by using Central Point Backup. No data recovery technique is foolproof. Making regular backups is your best protection against data loss.
- Run DiskFix regularly. DiskFix can detect and fix problems with your hard drive before they occur.
- Run Compress regularly. Compress eliminates file fragmentation. When you run Compress, your files are rearranged into contiguous segments on your hard drive. This makes them significantly easier to recover if they are accidentally deleted.
- Use System Information (SI) to print a report of your system configuration. The SI report provides important information about your hard drive, I/0 ports, interrupts and addresses, and more. Generate an SI report when you in-

stall PC Tools and anytime you change the configuration of your system, such as when you add hard drives, RAM memory, or expansion ports.

- Use PC Format to format disks. Unlike DOS, PC Format does not automatically wipe out existing data during formatting operations. Thus, if you accidentally format a disk, the data usually can be recovered by using Unformat.

Index

E

F

H

M

N

O

P

Q

R

S

T

U

V

W

X

Selections from The SYBEX Library

UTILITIES

The Computer Virus Protection Handbook
Colin Haynes
192pp. Ref. 696-0
This book is the equivalent of an intensive emergency preparedness seminar on computer viruses. Readers learn what viruses are, how they are created, and how they infect systems. Step-by-step procedures help computer users to identify vulnerabilities, and to assess the consequences of a virus infection. Strategies on coping with viruses, as well as methods of data recovery, make this book well worth the investment.

Mastering the Norton Utilities 5
Peter Dyson
400pp, Ref. 725-8
This complete guide to installing and using the Norton Utilities 5 is a must for beginning and experienced users alike. It offers a clear, detailed description of each utility, with options, uses and examples—so users can quickly identify the programs they need and put Norton right to work. Includes valuable coverage of the newest Norton enhancements.

Mastering PC Tools Deluxe 6 *For Versions 5.5 and 6.0*
425pp, Ref. 700-2
An up-to-date guide to the lifesaving utilities in PC Tools Deluxe version 6.0 from installation, to high-speed back-ups, data recovery, file encryption, desktop applications, and more. Includes detailed background on DOS and hardware such as floppies, hard disks, modems and fax cards.

Norton Desktop for Windows Instant Reference
Sharon Crawford
Charlie Russell
200pp; Ref. 894-7
For anyone using Norton's version of the Windows desktop, here's a compact, fast-access guide to every feature of the package—from file management functions, to disaster prevention tools, configuration commands, batch language extensions, and more. Concise, quick-reference entries are alphabetized by topic, and include practical tips and examples.

Norton Utilities 5 Instant Reference
Michael Gross
162pp. Ref. 737-1
Organized alphabetically by program name, this pocket-sized reference offers complete information on each utility in the Norton 5 package—including a descriptive summary, exact syntax, command line options, brief explanation, and examples. Gives proficient users a quick reminder, and helps with unfamiliar options.

Norton Utilities 6 Instant Reference
Michael Gross
175pp; Ref. 865-3
This pocket-size guide to Norton Utilities 6 provides fast answers when and where they're needed. Reference entries are organized alphabetically by program name, and provide a descriptive summary, exact syntax, command line options, brief explanations, and examples. For a quick reminder, or help with unfamiliar options.

PC Tools Deluxe 6 Instant Reference

Gordon McComb

194pp. Ref. 728-2

Keep this one handy for fast access to quick reminders and essential information on the latest PC Tools Utilities. Alphabetical entries cover all the Tools of Version 6—from data recovery to desktop applications—with concise summaries, syntax, options, brief explanations, and examples.

Understanding Norton Desktop for Windows

Peter Dyson

500pp; Ref. 888-2

This detailed, hands-on guide shows how to make the most of Norton's powerful Windows Desktop—to make Windows easier to use, customize and optimize the environment, take advantage of shortcuts, improve disk management, simplify disaster recovery, and more. Each program in the Norton Desktop gets thorough treatment, with plenty of practical examples.

Understanding the Norton Utilities 6 (Second Edition)

Peter Dyson

500pp; Ref. 855-6

Here is a detailed, practical sourcebook for PC users seeking to streamline their computing and extend the power of DOS with Norton 6. Features hands-on examples and up-to-date coverage of such topics as file management and security, hard disk maintenance, disaster recovery, and batch programming. Includes a complete command guide.

Understanding PC Tools 7

Peter Dyson

500pp; Ref. 850-5

Turn here for a complete guide to taking advantage of the new version of PC Tools for DOS 5 and Windows—with hands-on coverage of everything from installation to telecommunications. Special topics include networking; data security and encryption; virus detection; remote computing; and many new options for disk maintenance, disaster prevention, and data recovery.

Up & Running with Carbon Copy Plus

Marvin Bryan

124pp. Ref. 709-6

A speedy, thorough introduction to Carbon Copy Plus, for controlling remote computers from a PC. Coverage is in twenty time-coded "steps"—lessons that take 15 minutes to an hour to complete. Topics include program set-up, making and receiving calls, file transfer, security, terminal emulation, and using Scripts.

Up & Running with Norton Desktop for Windows

Michael Gross
David Clark

140pp; Ref. 885-8

Norton's new desktop utility package lets you customize Windows to your heart's content. Don't miss out! Learn to use this versatile program in just 20 basic lessons. Each lesson takes less than an hour to complete, and wastes no time on unnecessary detail.

Up & Running with Norton Utilities 5

Michael Gross

154pp. Ref. 819-0

Get a fast jump on Norton Utilties 5. In just 20 lessons, you can learn to retrieve erased files, password protect and encrypt your data, make your system work faster, unformat accidentally formatted disks, find "lost" files on your hard disk, and reconstruct damaged files.

Up & Running with Norton Utilities 6

Michael Gross

140pp; Ref. 874-2

Come up to speed with Norton Utilities 6 in just 20 steps. This slim volume covers all of Norton's constituent programs (for both versions 5 and 6), provides command line syntax and options, and spells out the differences between versions 5 and 6 with special upgrade notes.

PC Tools Commands by Task

Task	Command or Utility
Protect against viruses	VDefend (Part 3)
Protect deleted files	Data Monitor (Part 3)
Protect file with password	PC Secure (Part 3)
Rearrange files and directories on hard disk	Compress (Part 3)
Recover deleted file	Undelete (Part 3)
Recover formatted disk	Unformat (Part 3)
Remove memory-resident utilities	Kill (Part 3)
Rename file	Rename File (Part 1)
Report file and disk allocations	File Map, Disk Map (Part 1)
Report I/O port information	System Info (Part 1)
Report memory usage	Memory Map (Part 1)
Restrict access to commands	Change User Level, (Part 1)
Run programs from PC Shell	Run, Launch, Open (Part 1)
Schedule appointments	Appointment Scheduler (Part 2)
Schedule automated backups	CP Backup (Part 3)